THE PROMISE

Black Youth Confront the Cauldron of Apartheid

THE PROMISE

Black Youth Confront the Cauldron of Apartheid

> ## Vol. 1
> ### THE VIEW FROM BOPHELONG, SOUTH AFRICA

by

DONALD A. TSOLO

iUniverse, Inc.
New York   Bloomington

iUniverse books may be ordered through booksellers or by contacting:

iUniverse
1663 Liberty Drive
Bloomington, IN 47403
www.iuniverse.com
1-800-Authors (1-800-288-4677)

Because of the dynamic nature of the Internet, any Web addresses or links contained in this book may have changed since publication and may no longer be valid. The views expressed in this work are solely those of the author and do not necessarily reflect the views of the publisher, and the publisher hereby disclaims any responsibility for them.

ISBN: 978-1-4401-4540-7 (sc)
ISBN: 978-1-4401-4542-1 (dj)
ISBN: 978-1-4401-4541-4 (ebook)

Library of Congress Control Number: 2009929369

Printed in the United States of America

iUniverse rev. date: 07/02/2009

Acknowledgments

For a true story covering terrain as rocky and treacherous as apartheid South Africa, it is extremely difficult to isolate those one could define as leading contributors worthy of mention within the limits of an acknowledgment page. In spite of this, though, the following were more than helpful in providing assistance:

Richard P. Stevens, PhD, author of several books and articles on topics ranging from the Israeli-Palestinian conflict to intricate, detailed articles on a variety of African political developments. It was Dick who initiated the idea of a Lambretta scooter tour of central and eastern Africa that features significantly in this first of two volumes publication. It was also Dick who suggested substantial inclusion of graphics in the text and provided most of the safari-related pictures. That Dick is still a strong advocate of a pro-Africa American foreign policy and has a largely Sudanese extended family is a testimony to the depth of influence our stay in Lesotho had on our future.

Others I will always feel thankful for include:

H. George Henry, a Cuban-born economics professor who provided the VW buggy used during the Africa safari tour. George is now in blissful retirement in Florida.

The various functionaries at the Africa Desk of the U.S. State Department at that time, who facilitated the provision of all-inclusive scholarships for South African refugees and who helped my personal introduction to the Washington D.C. community and its liberal wing.

Assistance in the writing of the text was provided by the Writers Guild, The Plantation at Leesburg, Florida. Within this group was Joyce Halvorsen whose literary insights into the psyche of the American Indians enabled her to empathize with the victims of apartheid. She provided primary assistance with publication format issues.

Primary day-to-day support throughout the writing of this first of two volumes was provided by my wife and my in-laws. The ready hospitality provided by my in-laws during our frequent visits to their home in Orlando, Florida, has made their home our home away from home. I also was gratified that our friend

Sonia V. Gonsalves, PhD, with the support of her beloved husband, Conrad Dyer, PhD, visited South Africa.

Sonia assisted with authenticating some details of sections dealing with Bophelong and its environs and provided the colorful pictures of my permanent contribution to the Nhlapu Court, Bophelong, cul-de-sac: a huge, gravity-defying poplar in front of my parental residence.

Introduction

Donald Arnoldt Tseole Tsolo, nicknamed Phae Phae, pronounced Pye Pye, was born on a farm on the outskirts of Vereeniging, Republic of South Africa, May 1st 1939. The only person in attendance at his birth was his grandmother. The farm was owned by a white family with whom Phae's father had a share-crop agreement.

At seven years of age, Phae started attending school miles away from home. He had to walk to and from school—a distance in excess of ten miles—daily. In his first year of schooling, Phae witnessed an incident that was to determine his approach to studying and life: the sight of a child being whipped by the school principal for failing to do his homework. When he heard the reason for the whipping, he made a solemn promise to himself never to give any authority figure in the school system cause to whip him for not having done his homework. This book is in many ways a contextual study of the evolution and outcomes of this elementary school resolve.

The Promise is also an in-depth portrayal of the barbarism fathered by apartheid and how this barbarism radicalized some good-hearted, God-fearing Americans against apartheid. Some of the key Americans in this drama are still alive: Richard Paul Stevens is still actively involved in admirable acts of humanity and assistance to the people of the Sudan. He lives on the outskirts of Washington D.C., while H.

George Henry, the economist, is living in retirement at The Plantation at Leesburg, Florida.

Some of the Southern African characters in the book are also still alive: Barbara Masekela was up until recently the South African ambassador to the United States. Samuel Mokete Mosiea lives in the Washington D.C. area. Ndlozi Philemon Radebe lives in retirement in Sebokeng, South Africa. Elizabeth Ngee Khosana is still actively employed in the medical health field in the Evaton area, a few miles north of Sebokeng. Dido Diseko has a doctorate in electrical engineering and is still working for Eskom, the South African energy giant. Many of Phae's brothers and sisters are deceased, but Dr. Molupe Hendrik Tsolo is still manning his surgery in Sasolburg, often working well beyond 5 PM when necessary. Pauline, the firstborn sister, still resides in the wider Bophelong area.

As an in-depth portrayal of life under apartheid in the Vaal Triangle, this book is likely to be unsurpassed. Some scenes are so brutal that the author was seen shedding tears more than once while reading sections to audiences of book writers.

Readers are welcome to submit comments/questions to the author at Molupe@ icon.co.za.

Chapter I

It is terribly infuriating to be young, black, and poor in apartheid South Africa. It sometimes gnaws at your guts, forcing you to curse and swear and laugh with little or no provocation.

It was no wonder then that Phae Phae (pronounced Pye Pye, though most simply called him Phae) paused outside the kitchen doorway, surveyed the array of matchbox-like dwellings in front of him, and mused over the pros and cons of going to school. Not that he hated school. No, sir. Far from it. But this morning was different.

It was a bitterly cold winter morning exacerbated by the notorious Drakensberg winds howling dusty hell across the barren plains. On this godforsaken morning, with no cock, fowl, or dog in sight, Phae had to cycle to school miles away in an oversized, faded, tattered, and coarse World War II army overcoat. His bare toes were as exposed as the day he was first ushered unceremoniously into this world with the aid of an aged, leather-skinned grandmother on a farm bordering the Vaal River that was within sight of Vereeniging's Brick and Tile industrial complex. His vaselined, clean-shaven head boasted two thin tufts of hair just above the forehead—his rare concession to the fashionable. Taking a deep breath, Phae pulled his right arm from somewhere inside the army overcoat and gave his nose a good blowing while he pressed his thumb against his nostrils. The white mucous whizzed through the air and landed on some half-frozen dahlias. As soon as he completed this operation and finished musing, he swung his rickety bicycle eastward and pedaled away.

Coping with the bitterly cold wintry days of the Bophelong area are Sonia Gonsalves, New Jersey, USA, and Phae's relative, Masebupi Lydia Monaheng, firstborn in Jeremiah's family line.

Needless to say, he was an unimpressive figure as he cycled through the maze of footpaths linking black Bophelong with affluent, white, and ultraconservative Vanderbijl Park. Phae had to use the side paths; it was safer that way. There was no need to confront the forces of law and order so early on a Monday morning. He knew one of two things could land him behind prison bars.

First, his bicycle did not meet township standards. It was defective in almost every way you could imagine: tires with multiple bulging patches, wheels with several spokes missing or loose, and no lights, bells, or brakes. Still, the machine worked, and when he rode downhill, it gave Phae the exhilarating feeling of bursting through the sound barrier. The second thing that could land him in trouble with the cops was the old matter of the reference book. The Verwoerd government and its post-World War II predecessors had decided that all blacks—

Bantu or Kaffir in Afrikaner parlance—had to carry reference books, often called passes, at all times to indicate that they were entitled to reside outside the government-decreed official areas of permanent residence for the different tribal groups of the country: Bantustans. Phae had nothing against this law if only God or Verwoerd could give him pants with pockets to accommodate the multi-paged identity document. As things stood, he had lost his reference book twice and was now dead-scared to appear before the awe-inspiring majesty in the Natives/Naturelle Commissioner's office. So, there you are, vulnerable Phae, hit the bypaths and thank God that there were not enough policemen and their Alsatian dogs to seal off this escape route.

Passing Vanderbijl Park, the rickety Phillips shot toward Sharpeville. A cluster of trees divided black Sharpeville from Vanderbijl Park. Negotiating his way through this thicket always gave Phae the creeps, like watching a Frankenstein-like monster emerge from some ancient tomb.

What gave Phae the creeps this time, though, was not the spookiness of the place, even though it boasted a segregated cemetery nearby, but the remote possibility of bumping into a contingent of the benzene-inhaling Sharpeville teenage gangs who were reputed to hate the upstart, up-country, rustic but pushy Bophelong boys. A lonely encounter with this gang could be a messy affair.

With his face now ashen grey, his cheeks spattered with salty drying tears, and his lips, fingers, and toes almost frostbitten, Phae shot through urbane but simmering Sharpeville. Beyond this he had to cycle through the commercial, industrial, and residential complexes of sleepy Afrikaner white Vereeniging. Once beyond these, he swung northwestward to the dusty-smelling shacks of Vereeniging's poorer, doomed black section—Top Location—and his destination, the Lekoa Shandu High School. Upon arrival at the school, he jammed his heel against the Phillips's rear tire, and the bicycle screeched to a dusty halt. "Thank goodness," he murmured to himself. One more trying journey was over, and now there was one more ghastly day to be faced—and this without delay he mused.

It was, in fact, to be a ghastly but not, for the most part, atypical winter day at school. For starters, Phae was late. The authoritarian headmaster and his equally authoritarian staff had already held and dismissed the compulsory morning assembly. For a split second, Phae pictured what the assembly gathering resembled: rows of students in their uniforms. The girls would have worn nice, clean, starched white blouses and blue tunics. The boys most likely wore short khaki pants and khaki shirts. Shoes were few and far between—most students were barefooted. Some girls clutched their berets and books tightly against their chests to ensure warmth and compliance with regulations. For boys, caps and the tam-like "copperheads" were scarcer still. Teachers' attire was invariably strictly formal. The whole assembly proceedings, including hymns, prayer, a short sermon, and announcements, were conducted with stilted formality and verbosity. It was a rule savagely enforced throughout the proceedings that the students maintain silence— complete, utter, and absolute. Immediate administration of corporal punishment followed any unauthorized deviations.

A Lekoa Shandu High School student from Sharpeville. Picture taken two years after high school.

Phae never forgot the consequences of last month's deviation from assembly silence. How it happened no one knows for sure. Suffice it to say, while the headmaster was proclaiming: "By the powers invested in me, by the school board, and the government, I wish to …" one of the boys was heard to say: "He has shaved his goatee!" The remark sparked the most spontaneous outburst of giggles that spread like wildfire across the rows of students. The principal's fury was unleashed as he advanced toward the students with cane in hand and shirt, tie, and coat a-flying. He lashed blindly at the students until, in apparent exhaustion, a male colleague helped him to his office.

For Phae, though, this was a badly chosen time for reminiscing.

Showing more audacity than caution, he locked up his Phillips and dashed toward the classroom with knowing stealth. The corridors and veranda couldn't have been more empty or quiet. The classroom door was closed. To Phae this was awkward and maybe intimidating. He paused, undecided as what to do. Knocking meant disturbing whatever routine was going on inside. Simply opening the door and waltzing in might appear disrespectful and unnecessarily conceited. He stole a quick glance toward the principal's office and then pleaded to the heavens above for intercession. Getting no reasonably encouraging nod from either source, he decided on a unilateral course. Pressing his right hand on the doorknob, he gave it a twist and a nearly imperceptible push. The door opened, revealing a sight that was not totally unexpected. All the students were lined up against the walls. Toward the far end of the room, the teacher, a white Afrikaner, stood with his cane lifted high above his shoulders in readiness to strike a boy who had forgotten that "33 and 1/3" of a pound sterling was six shillings and eight pence in British imperial sterling currency.

This was a "mental arithmetic" period. The answer had to be ready in seconds otherwise you simply stretched out your hand for whipping. This was the fate about to visit the poor trembling boy in front of the teacher. With instinctive protectiveness, Phae slammed the door hard enough to give the boy a chance by diverting the teacher's attention. The desired diversion was achieved with unfortunate consequences for Phae.

"Donald!" the teacher roared in a voice of doom, using Phae's official name and petrifying all his students. "Stand against the blackboard!" Phae moved with uncharacteristic clumsiness. From the back of the class the voice of authority boomed again. "Put down your books and coat and stand against the wall with your back touching the blackboard…. Stretch your arms above your shoulders!" The words fell out of the authority's mouth with such rapidity, Phae hesitated to move.

"Sir, but sir," he almost whispered.

"Don't sir me, boy. Move!" the voice of authority shot back.

Phae took his position as ordered, and the orgy of "mental arithmetic," questioning, whipping, guessing, and fumbling continued until it was forcefully terminated by the bell announcing the end of the period.

With "mentals" over, the teacher turned toward Phae. Moving rapidly, he managed to disguise his age and physical condition. Tall, lean, and hungry-looking, his mouth was just a slit that hardly, if ever, opened to reveal his tobacco-stained teeth. Needless to say, he never smiled in class. With eyes curiously suggestive of the Orient and ears uprightly cat-like, he looked positively otherworldly and intimidating to Phae. How this repulsive creature ever found his way into a black classroom was to Phae a mystery wrapped in an enigma. He braced himself for questioning and was not disappointed.

"Donald, my boy," droned the teacher, "you know you are late?"

"Yes, sir!" Phae replied, as creeping anger warmed his frost-riddled toes and fingers.

"Now, my boy, as punishment for your lateness, you are to stay in the classroom during recess and the lunch hour. During that lunch hour, you are to complete exercises one to ten on page forty-nine of your arithmetic textbook. Is that clear?"

"No, sir," replied Phae, confidence slowly returning to his crispy voice.

"No, sir? My foot! What's wrong with you, boy? Do you want me to whip you here and now?"

"No, sir!" Phae pleadingly replied.

"Then get your foolish black face off my blackboard. Move!" His slit-like mouth seemed like a gash that was poised to spout poison.

Phae, realizing the futility of resistance, collected his belongings and moved to his desk. With that confrontation mitigated, a visible, almost tangible relief settled over the class. As if marking a closure, some students cast Phae understanding smiles. The relief, however, was short-lived.

The next period was the dreaded Afrikaans language. To the Lekoa Shandu High School students, Afrikaans was dominantly, if not exclusively, the language of the minority Boers—descendants of the Dutch who were granted transient grazing rights along the Cape coast in the seventeenth century by the native citizens of the area that history now calls the Cape Province of South Africa.

The Boers unilaterally converted temporary guest land rights into permanent God-decreed real estate rights with inevitable consequences characterized by unending brutal clashes. Along the frontiers of confrontation, the Dutch language was modified by the dictates of isolation into a new language that revealed the contradictions that were to bedevil southern Africa. The modified Dutch language came to be called Afrikaans and its speakers Afrikaners.

Common sense suggests that Afrikaner translates to African in English, but an Afrikaner wouldn't buy that logic. And as if in retaliation, the Africans would not accept Afrikaans as a language worth studying. Those who conversed in Afrikaans often did so when their intentions were either not honorable or were blatantly criminal. In time, the latter users came to be known as the "Tsotsis." Neither Phae nor any of his classmates wished to be identified, even remotely, with either Tsotsism or Afrikaans—a fact the apartheid establishment either refused or failed to acknowledge. Instead, the establishment elevated Afrikaans to the dazzling heights of South Africa's official language as a necessary corollary to triumphant Boer nationalism.

With an appointed board to supervise its growth, Afrikaans was now a required subject in all African schools. And who was to teach Afrikaans to the African children? Afrikaners, of course. Was it any wonder then that the compulsory teaching of Afrikaans in schools for black children was met by a resistance that was deep and profound and in time bloody and fateful?

The Lekoa Shandu High School students, unable to launch any major offensive against the compulsory teaching of an alien and hated language, opted for the one counteroffensive they could mount— refusal to acquire written or spoken fluency in Afrikaans. As if in response to this deep-seated hatred of Afrikaans, the teacher shifted the Afrikaans period from a study of the mechanics of language and the dynamics of communication to a stifling obsession with memorizing poetry and prose selections in Afrikaans. Every week students were to select either a poem or prose selection of their choice and to "nicely, carefully, and artistically" enter the same in their Afrikaans anthology exercise books. Each entry had to be laid out in such a way as to allow adequate space for the student to mount a picture or a hand drawing of a significant aspect of the poem or prose selection.

Clippings had to be meticulously cut, centered, and mounted

on the page facing the selection. An appropriate caption or heading also had to be provided by the student. Below the picture or drawing, a relevant quote from the selection had to be entered to supposedly cement and/or demonstrate the student's comprehension of the text. Most Afrikaans periods were taken up by students working on their anthologies and laboriously trying to meet the demanding specifications of their teacher. Needless to say, a large number of the pictures chosen by the students to illustrate aspects of their prose or poems selections were rejected by the teacher for one reason or another. To increase the likelihood of the teacher accepting their selections, students had to bring large numbers of them and hope that at least one would meet the teacher's strict requirements. The student who was most keen to please the teacher on this score was a young, sensitive, and diminutive girl from Sharpeville. The girls called her Jane, though her official registry entry read: Janette Cinaphe Zulu.

Jane had chosen a fairly short poem for this week with an innocuous theme: a mosquito being chased by humans. Jane personally hated mosquitoes. There was nothing praiseworthy about their color, shape, or size. Worse, they were killers. Jane knew the connection between malaria deaths and mosquito bites. To comply with the teacher's stipulations, Jane had collected half a dozen different sized color pictures of mosquitoes and was yearning to mount one of these in her exercise book. Experience had taught her the wisdom of checking with the teacher before mounting her choice. "This should not be complicated," Jane thought. Her thoughts seemed, for a while, justified, but she soon stumbled upon a "Catch 22." There was only one assured route to resolve this: get the teacher's help.

"Sir. Sir, please!" she called, pushing her way through a thin cluster of pupils surrounding Authority's desk. The others easily gave way to Jane's enthusiastic, pleading tones. Soon it was Jane's turn to talk to the teacher.

"Sir! Sir!!" Her voice quivered. "I have found several beautiful pictures of mosquitoes." Without waiting for her teacher's response she continued. "Look at this one," she said. "Isn't it beautiful? I just adore the colors! Look at this one. You can see the body, the head ... don't you like it?"

"Janette Zulu!" the cold voice of authority cut in, "the beauty of your pictures is not my concern. Do you understand? I am not here to discuss that."

"But, sir, I don't want an ugly mosquito in my anthology book," Janette pleaded.

"Janette, that's not my concern. It's yours," he responded.

"My poem deals with mosquitoes, Sir!" Janette fired back. "I just need to get a mosquito to illustrate my poem and this is a beautiful mosquito picture," she insisted, failing completely to detect the disinterest of her teacher.

"Janette, your poem does not just deal with mosquitoes. It deals with mosquitoes being chased by a man. Do you follow me? Now, I want a picture of a mosquito being chased by a man. Do you follow me?" he fired back with a definitive tone.

"What does a mosquito being chased by a man look like?" Janette pleaded in a tone so subdued it was almost inaudible.

"Janette, that is your problem," he replied. "Next!" With that, Authority, whose actual name was Vander Merwe, dismissed the only bubbling enthusiast in the Afrikaans class. Other students were dismissed with mechanical swiftness and precision as picture clippings, photographs, and hand drawings found their way into Vander Merwe's wastepaper basket.

The history period was a classic of the Vander Merwe tradition. The subject was made to order: Piet Retief—the man who led the Afrikaners out of the Cape Province to escape control by the British in the 1830s—ended up at Dingaan's (the king of the Zulus) palace. The glee in the teacher's face told all those who cared: I love this subject and I am prepared. In no time, Vander Merwe produced from the desk drawer colorful but tattered charts showing Piet Retief's route, from the Cape to the Zulu kingdom in Natal. From the same source, he also produced diagrams of Voortrekker wagons and artists' renditions of Retief and his cohorts at Dingaan's palace gates.

Vander Merwe's enthusiasm and exuberance were self-evident as he dove into spirited descriptions of innocent, God-appointed agents of civilization, "our forefathers" as he sometimes referred to them, marching into Dingaan's palace—or, in Vander Merwe phraseology, kraal—with Bible in hand and goodwill in their hearts.

Phae listened to the lecture with contemptuous indifference. It was a story that had been retold from class to class and year to year. Worse yet, come Voortrekker Day in December, a guy couldn't move for fear of being caught by marauding gangs of Piet Retief's descendants. That soliloquy about Bible in hand and goodwill in their hearts jerked him up. He had never heard that one before.

"Wait a minute," he burst out with involuntary abruptness. "What's that you said?"

Vander Merwe stopped. His face reddened with incipient fury. Phae's question and tone had all the damnable ingredients for trouble. In spite of what appeared to be its virginal innocence and spontaneity, it had avoided any mention of "sir" in its directness and had stopped Vander Merwe at a point in his thinking where politics-sourced traditional Afrikaner orthodoxy had tempted him to deviate from the historical facts he knew so well. Resisting fury's imperatives with uncharacteristic deliberateness, Vander Merwe pulled out a white handkerchief and wiped his creased, steaming forehead.

"Repeat the question," he ordered with unexpected mildness. The mildness proved eufunctional. It gave Phae a crucial opportunity to de-escalate the situation by reframing his question.

"Sir, could you please repeat what you said about Piet Retief entering Dingaan's palace gates with Bible in hand and goodwill in his heart. I am afraid I missed something there."

Vander Merwe was pleased with Phae's rephrased question and its apparent genuineness. It offered both an escape from confrontation's inevitable path.

"Thank you," Vander Merwe answered as the faintest flicker of a smile momentarily hovered on the edges of his slit-like mouth. "My students," he continued, "when dealing with our eh … mmm! When dealing with history at certain higher levels, you are allowed some amount of scholarly license, something akin to poetic license, which enables you to reconstruct events in such a way as to make new interpretations possible." He noticed that he was losing his audience faster than was expedient, and he changed gears. "Now, Fowler and Smith, the advanced textbook some of you are using, does not contain enough for you to reconstruct and interpret material." Realizing that this tactic was still not breaking down any barriers, he decided to conclude, "In fact, even if it did, you are academically underequipped to independently make original reinterpretations."

The relevance of this to Phae was dubious to the point of being nonexistent. He, however, preferred not to overstretch his luck. This was not the case though with Joshua, the jet-black rotund boy from Tsirela, a black township lying between Vanderbijl Park and Evaton. Long an accomplished combatant in school debates, his face shone with positive glee at the possibility of a verbal scrimmage.

"Please, sir!" announced Joshua, his hand held high in the air in compliance with classroom protocol.

"Yes, Joshua Ngwenya," answered the teacher, uncertain what to expect.

"I still don't see how you can reinterpret a gun into a Bible or a treaty written in Dutch and agreed to by an unschooled illiterate into goodwill," Joshua proceeded. The provocative comment found its mark, and Vander Merwe knew the battle lines were defining themselves faster and sharper than his Calvinistic zeal had anticipated. To throw away the scabbard now would be foolhardy, he told himself. Complete retraction was more defensible and expedient. It also must be done without it being seen as defeat.

"This discussion," Vander Merwe addressed the class, "is veering too far from the topic for today. So I will advise that for the time being we accept the chain of events as painted by Fowler and Smith.

"It's obviously and understandably difficult for young minds to grasp the true meaning of historical interpretation and reconstruction," he concluded as the class breathed a sigh of relief.

The morning recess was far from lonely for Phae. In fact, confining him to the classroom during recess this time of the year was not really a punishment to him. The cold, blistering winds kept more than half of the class indoors anyhow. A few braved the weather and rushed to the bathrooms and were soon back. Fewer still went beyond the school gates to the neighboring Indian-owned shops to buy snacks, especially the highly affordable "magwenya," a homemade sweet, and tasty johnnycakes retailing at a penny each. Available fruits were imported and expensive this time of the year. Oranges, for example, sold at two for a "tickey," or three pence.

With Authority away in the staff room, classroom conversation became lively. Joshua, fresh from what he esteemed was a creditable performance against Vander Merwe, was whistling complacently to himself while bouncing a tennis ball—previously immersed overnight in kerosene to give it extra buoyancy—against a wall. Jane, true to her colors, never gave up figuring out how a mosquito being chased by a man would look like, and was now flipping through local magazines for mosquito pictures matching her subject: a mosquito being chased by a man. Toward the center of the classroom was a group of boys excitedly recounting last week's adventures.

"Boy!" one of them exclaimed, "I saw the white boys coming down the long driveway with dogs and sticks. As they rapidly got closer, I said to myself, 'Philemon, my dear boy, today you are done for. If they ever catch sight of you and your pocketful of stolen peaches, you are one heap of a dead son of a gun.' I clung tightly to the tree branch and held my breath while eyeing over and above me, nice, juicy, ripe peaches ready for the picking."

"Come quick, man! What did you then do?" one of the boys asked impatiently.

"What did I do? What do you mean what did I then do? You tell me. What would you do?" Philemon asked with marked hostility, as he suspected that someone was questioning his bravery.

"Leave him alone, Philemon, and continue. It's getting late. We soon have to rush back to the classroom," a usually taciturn Isaac cut in.

"How far were you from the fence marking the boundaries of the white people's plot?" a voice asked from the outer edges of the small group.

"I was ten peach tree rows from the fence," Philemon answered, adding, "from where I was, I could not see the fence marking the bounds of the property, but I knew if I rushed for it I had no chance of reaching it with those Rhodesian ridgebacks after me. So, boy, I just held on tight and prayed for God to help me, just this one time."

The picture of tall, thin Philemon clutching a peach tree trunk, his pockets bulging with stolen peaches while asking for God's help was truly bizarre but especially to young Sixpence, whose mirth couldn't resist exploding. His laughter was infectious, and he soon had everybody reeling in accompaniment. Seconds before the bell announcing the end of recess rang, Vander Merwe was back in the classroom—all of him, including cane and a bunch of teaching aids. The rush to get seated and ready for the next period caused momentary disarray as desks and chairs squeaked into position. For some unknown reason, the class seemed fascinated by the next lesson period, which was supposed to be a geography class with Northern Rhodesia as the topic. The source of the fascination could have been any of several.

First, the black Rhodesians, soon to be called Zimbabweans, the students had encountered were intriguing. With their strange language and politeness, they did not fit any category of people the students were familiar with. To the students, the Rhodesians in South Africa hovered in an in-between world in South Africa's racial and tribalistic mosaic. Their official designation as "foreign natives" did not help either.

Even more confusing to the students were reports in the media frequently hinting at uprisings and strikes in the Copper Belt led by an organization headed by one Kenneth Kaunda, a guitar-playing Pan Africanist. The students were not clear what Kaunda's short-term objectives were, but they all embraced reports of his call for an Africa free of colonialism and an independent North Rhodesia. These newspaper reports, sometimes accompanied by pictures of a fiery Kaunda addressing a rally, added mystique to an already fascinating region.

Of all the region's fascinations, the famous Victoria Falls were second to none. Few of the students had either seen or dreamt of visiting the Victoria Falls astride the Zambezi River. However, all of them had varying visions of its power and beauty. Was it not true that Dr. David Livingstone, supposedly the first white person to have seen the falls, thought they were a sight so beautiful that God's angels must have beheld them in their flight? Wasn't it equally true that the falls were classified as one of the world's wonders?

With Boorish inscrutability, Vander Merwe confined himself to the strict geographic facts about Northern Rhodesia: its position in central Africa, including the lines of longitude and latitude defining it, and the hard facts regarding the country's topography, crops, vegetation, minerals, towns, cities, and communication routes—including highways and railways. Since this was a double period, it meant ninety minutes of unpardonable folly, during which the hiatus between the students' interest and the teacher's obsession with facts hovered like an oppressive fog over the class. From an apparently polluted if not poisoned learning atmosphere, the sound of the lunchtime-break bell was more than welcome. It was salvation! After all, there was nothing exciting about learning the dry fact that Northern Rhodesia is an ancient, denuded plateau from four thousand to four thousand five hundred feet above sea level. And yet there is a wealth of exciting insights to glean from its people's fears, ambitions, struggles, and traditions. This was a world with which the students could identify and sympathize, and sometimes recoil from.

As soon as the necessary permission was granted for the students to leave the classroom, pandemonium broke loose. The boys whistled in joyous ecstasy, while some girls broke into cheerful, spontaneous singing. There was an exhilarating atmosphere amidst the din and confusion. It swept everybody in its wake. To these feelings and this spectacle, Vander Merwe was a rank and loathsome outsider. He chose to deliberately turn away from student activity and concentrated his blue eyes on something he saw through the high but dusty windows. The girls, as if in silent conspiracy to block him out, burst into a spontaneous song with undeniable political undertones:

> Koloi ena, ha ena mabili.
> Koloi ena, ha ena mabili.
> Sutha, sutha, uena Verwoerd
> Ha o sa suthi e ea ho thula ...

> This wagon (i.e., nationalism) has no wheels
> This wagon has no wheels
> Give way, give way, you Verwoerd,
> Unless you give way, you are going to be swept away.

(*Verwoerd* is the Afrikaner architect of apartheid.)

By the time the singing died down only two souls were left in the classroom—Vander Merwe and Phae. The former was still presumably hypnotized by the view out the window, while Phae, victim and victor, slowly and deliberately organized his desk as decreed by authority.

There was a calculated coldness in his movements and bearing. With head erect, shoulders flung back, and chest pushed outward, Phae started working on his assignments and did not stop until he finished, several minutes ahead of schedule. As soon as his assignments were done, he marched to the teacher's desk and presented his exercise book with a nonchalance that declared: I dare you to find a single mistake.

Vander Merwe read the signals well. He didn't bother to correct Phae's work. All he said was, "Okay, Donald, you may go for lunch now." If Vander Merwe had expected Phae to jump at this offer, he had misjudged his student. The khaki-clad boy turned to face him and, unperturbed, replied, "Not now, thanks!" He then proceeded to his desk for more self-generated schoolwork.

Vander Merwe felt like cursing the earth he stood on. He reddened, half-choked, swallowed, and strutted out of the classroom. Seconds later Phae followed, his face shining with victorious boyish malice.

There was never a dull lunch hour at the Lekoa Shandu High School. To the boys from outside Top Location, this was the hour when they all hopped on their myriad colored bicycles and raced to the stores to buy their lunches. The stores could not have been more than a fraction of a mile away, but the speeds the bikes reached in those short distances were astonishing. The excitement created by racing speeds, however, did not come close to equaling the excitement generated by the skills the riders displayed in applying all sorts of nonconventional braking tricks—including the use of their bare heels. In this case, the rider would slam his heels against the rear tire, which forced the bike to screech to a dusty halt. Other skills the boys displayed included standing on top of their bikes while riding at full speed. Cornering and turning without using hands seemed to fascinate most. Their performances were invariably more creative when girls were watching.

Lunch was simple. Most of the children were happy with two slices of whole wheat bread served with peanut butter and jam that was washed down with a soda. When one's pockets were, for one reason or another, deeper than usual, lunch might include a dessert. After eating, the students had limited options: take a girl on a short walk or play soccer. Lunchtime soccer was nothing fancy. For starters, the soccer balls were actually tennis balls that had been previously soaked overnight in kerosene. This stripped them of their fuzz and left them slightly bigger and definitely more bouncy. The higher the ball bounced, the greater the owner's glory resounded. Goal posts were improvised and consisted usually of two stones set ten to fifteen feet apart.

The position of goalkeeper was the least popular since it provided minimal activity. Frequently the position was not manned for lack of players. Whatever the status at the goal posts, the enthusiasm of the participants was never dampened. Expertise in play among these boys would have pleased Pele. You name the soccer movement, and these boys would execute it in colorful style. No wonder it was often said that obsession with style was the bane of local soccer.

Those who were not actively engaged in play were frequently found along the sides of the local buildings that faced the sun. Here, protected from the winds and warmed by the sun, the students would have some of their most intimate conversational moments. In one corner, a group of boys and girls were discussing an absorbing topic.

"Imagine, Joyce," Helen remarked. "Philemon's sister is going to be married."

"To whom?" Joyce asked, not fully grasping the importance of Helen's announcement.

"What's that you said, Helen?" a boy demanded from somewhere in the back of the group.

"I said Philemon's sister is going to be married," Helen replied.

"I can't believe it. No! No! No! Can you imagine what's going to happen to her?" the boy asked, walking to the front of the congregation where a small mound added a few inches to his height with the accompanying advantage of commanding the audience's attention.

"What's going to happen? Come, do tell us, seeing as to how you know so much about these things," one girl demanded.

"Eh, you want me to tell you?" the orator replied. "Boy, all I know is that the moment she gets married she is lost. Next thing she hears from him is do this, do that, give me this, and give me that," he added.

"There's no way that's going to happen to my sister, boy!" another person exclaimed.

"Imagine, she has to sleep with him every night," another boy said, challenging the small crowd's imagination before posing a revealing question. "And what do you think they will be doing together in bed every night? I hate to think of it!"

The idea of Philemon's sister sleeping with her husband on the same bed every night seemed to be the funniest thing this bunch of kids had ever heard. Someone chuckled at the thought. Chuckles graduated into giggling, and from giggling some of the boys and girls burst into almost uncontrollable fits of laughter.

In yet another corner, there was a cluster of boys who were discussing boxing. With the upcoming Sharpeville versus Bophelong amateur boxing tournament around the corner, speculation as to who was going to win was rampant.

"I am sure Bophelong is going to win. I know those boys, and they are good," remarked a young fellow from Tsirela.

"No, you are making a mistake, Peter," answered Themba. "Sharpeville is the better side. Look at it this way: the Sharpeville boys have lots of experience. They have good supervision, high popularity among sports reporters, and maybe more importantly, they are disciplined."

"What makes you think Bophelong has no discipline or experience?" Peter fired back.

"I have seen them fight several times, all over the region, from here to Pretoria and Parys, and I bet you they have as much experience as the Sharpeville boys," Peter concluded.

"If you are going to talk that way, you are wasting our time," cut in Philemon of peach-stealing infamy. "In boxing," he continued, his voice getting louder and more impatient. "In boxing, it is not the team that matters in a tournament. It is the individual boxer who matters above everything else. When you are in that ring, you are facing one man, not a team," he concluded.

"What are you suggesting, Philemon?" somebody asked.

"I am suggesting that you should compare boxer to boxer and weight to weight. For example, it's a question of how the Bophelong flyweight division hopes, what's his name, the short Xhosa-speaking boy?" asked Philemon, pausing for help.

"Fanyana!" a voice offered.

"Fanyana, yes, that's him," Philemon said, looking in the direction where that help had come from. "It's a question of how Fanyana will perform against Isaac Thapedi," he continued. "Isaac uses a sharp, crisp, short jab followed by a right hook. In fact, it's often two quick jabs followed by a left uppercut and a right cross. That's a hell of a combination. Fanyana, on the other hand, rains his blows from long range. He just punches continuously, like a piston-firing machine." He concluded with a look suggesting that he thought he had made a good case.

"So, who do you think is going to win between those two?" asked the Tsirela boy, eager for definite guidelines.

"Hell, man, think it out for yourself," someone advised.

"I don't want to think it out for myself when it comes to those two," the unidentified boy answered. "I simply wish to know who is it Philemon picks to win."

"Okay, I'll tell you what," Philemon fired back, his batteries recharged. "Fanyana is going to whip Isaac well and good. I can see it now. Fanyana will be standing in a couched position and raining straight punches from the shoulders. Isaac will run around the ring a few times trying jabs until Fanyana catches up with him, and then...!"

"Stop that nonsense, Philemon!" remarked a new voice. "You ought to know better than that!"

"Better than what?" someone else impatiently cut in.

"Better than pick Fanyana as the winner. He is just a raw kid from the Bantustans," the new voice answered, with an almost paternalistic concern. "In boxing," the voice continued, "it is not rained blows that win a fight. No! The decisive punches are short, accurately placed, and solid. Worse, my dear friend, Fanyana's punches do not land on the knuckles, but on the inside of the glove."

"Yes, that sounds true," somebody declared.

"It doesn't sound true, it is true you fool!" answered a new, bellicose figure waving a stick. "Boxing is a science—a science of movement, speed, and accuracy. And that's not learned while cultivating corn or herding cattle."

"Let's duck that flyweight scene," Peter suggested. "It does not make much sense wasting a good lunch hour on flyweights. It's the bantams, featherweights, and the lightweights that excite me, boy! There you have speed, punching power, and a whole heap of knockouts. The higher and heavier weights are dull. I don't care a farthing for them," Peter concluded, all gung-ho for action.

"For the time being, though, you better settle with the flyweights,

Peter," Philemon cautioned. Changing gears, he added, "I have just heard the bell and, if I were you, I would start moving." He dashed out of the circle en route to the classroom and Vander Merwe.

Within what Peter calls "two shakes of a duck's tail" everybody was gone, leaving only food crumbs and footprints as a reminder of what had been for lunch.

The Vereeniging-Vanderbijl Park area was prone to rapid weather changes—including unforeseen and unannounced damaging wind storms. Originating from somewhere in the Lesotho mountains or the Orange Free State—dry, sandy waste lands—the feared twister roared toward Top Location, spinning, twisting, and curling in its fiercely snake-like course. Crossing over Vereeniging, it whipped up the town's garbage, dead leaves, and dust into one whirling fury.

Sensing danger, dogs, cats, chickens, and other domestic livestock dashed for cover. Youngsters, frightened off their playing fields, scrambled for safety. In their scramble, though, some remembered a traditional twist for those confronted by wind fury: spit at the twister while declaring, in all solemnity: "Ha e ee Matebeleng—let it go to the lands of the Ndebeles!"

No one knows for sure if nature ever gave a nod to this invocation in the past, but it was unlikely to now comply; with rapid detribalization and urbanization, it might be tricky for a twister to locate the Ndebeles. Unable to divert the monster, the youngsters ran for indoor cover.

The twister hit Top Location in its vulnerable belly in the southwest, where ramshackle shelters disintegrated with dramatic suddenness in its wake. Sheds of all descriptions, corrugated iron sheets once used for roofing, pots and pans, beds and blankets, all were torn from their diverse moorings and tossed into a twirling vortex. From the southwest the twister took the remainder of Top Location in an arc-like embrace before it zeroed on its most regrettable target: the high school.

Seconds before the twister struck, there was an eerie silence in the classroom. During that most unnatural silence, Phae cast a glance toward Vander Merwe and noticed, frightfully, a most disturbing twist of Vander Merwe's mouth slit accompanied by a rapid alternating reddening and paling of his bizarre visage. Phae's glance changed into a fixed concentration when some force seemed to jerk Vander Merwe upright, petrified and benumbed, into the path of the oncoming fury. When the class noticed the spectacle, hell broke loose.

No one quite knew what hit Vander Merwe, but there he lay—big, white, and prostrate. The silenced Authority, now a pallid fragility, greeted the other students as they slowly emerged from their hiding places and scrambled for their possessions. For them, unfortunately, there was nothing much to salvage.

All manner of student gear—texts, lined exercise books, rulers—were either swept outside in tatters or lay strewn all over the floor. Student coats, hats, and berets were either missing or misplaced. While the classroom door seemed intact, the same couldn't be said of the windows. Most were torn from their hinges and had been either flung away or now hung loose. The classroom's veranda, torn from its supporting pillars, now stood angular and twisted, a supplicant to unknown powers.

Phae, resisting an impulse to dash for his bicycle, stood up, saw Vander Merwe, and almost collapsed in fright. Regaining his posture, he moved with a new sense of determination and purpose to where the silent Vander Merwe lay. Instinctively, he gently placed his hand on the white man's face. A certified CPR administrant, Phae knew what to look for. Touching the face would at best yield temperature readings but would otherwise not be too useful. He decided to follow standard routines for the situation and checked for breathing and heartbeat. The findings were negative.

"He's dead!" Phae exclaimed. "I think Vander Merwe is dead." He looked among the scared classmates for somebody he could trust to execute the next step: informing the principal, who would then activate the town's rescue squad. He chose Philemon and gave the order: "Philemon, run to the office and tell the principal that Vander Merwe is showing no signs of breathing or heartbeat. Tell the principal to immediately call for an emergency rescue squad ambulance."

Philemon tore out of the classroom toward the principal's office, hurriedly skirting the debris strewn all over the assembly grounds. He must have found the principal sooner than expected, and within what appeared to be only minutes the place was afire with police, an ambulance, and concerned parents. Among the parents was an aged lady leaning on a cane with a handle carved like the head of a cobra. She was heard to sigh, "What a way to hell!" as the ambulance crew whisked stretchered Vander Merwe away.

Chapter 2

The merciless winter season continued in its inexorable path. With its frequent blasts of bitterly cold, dusty winds, frost and light snow, it devastated the countryside as far as the eye could see. Man, land, and beast suffered, but to what extent? Indisputably, the perception of the severity of the cold was directly related to the circumstances of individual families. Ironically, to those living in traditional thatched roof houses, indoors were warmer, particularly following the evening indoor "mbaola"—improvised but highly functional wood-and-coal-burning heating and cooking devises. With their thick heat-absorbing walls, traditional structures forced the heat to linger longer. To those living in supposedly more modern burnt brick or cinder block houses with corrugated iron roofs but without insulation or central heating, the impact of the cold was harsh. Those who suffered the full brunt of the winter were the shack dwellers, whether in Top Location or Evaton. In their case, there was little to mitigate the extremities of nature.

Mid-year school breaks occurred before mid-winter. All the kids looked forward to the school breaks, and Phae was no exception. He loved being home, winter or summer. During either season he had self-generated pat projects. For this winter break, he had offered to complete two projects. First, he would paint the interior walls of the Nhlapo Court parental residence. Second, he would continue preparing the garden for next season's crops. Phae called winter outdoor chores at home "a piece of cake." In the absence of a winter vegi-culture, maintaining the garden consisted largely of sweeping away dead leaves from underneath the scattered fruit trees that he had planted. Unlike some families, however, Phae did not burn the debris but swept it to the far end of the garden where it was added to his compost heap.

Indoor house painting wasn't a piece of cake. There were just too many variables that impacted the project, from smoke on the kitchen walls to loose old paint in other rooms that had to be peeled off. Before peeling and repainting, Phae had the exasperating task of covering furniture, carpets, and other valuable surfaces to protect them from either dust or paint sprays. Another simple annoyance in indoor painting was making sure the separation line where two colors meet was sharply defined. Even though Phae knew the difficulties of indoor painting, he still had the guts to promise his father that his painting performance would be the pride of the family. Painting was a two-stage operation. The first stage was simple: use a primer. The second stage proved taxing, especially since his mom, dad, and sisters had different ideas as to what colors or shades they wanted. Once the issue of the exact color shades to use was settled, everything moved swiftly and the whole operation was over within two weeks. In celebration, Phae spent an entire Saturday at the local soccer and tennis fields having the time of his life. The celebrations continued into the next day, a Sunday.

The last Sunday of winter was Phae's special day. It marked the end of the winter chores season for him. He approached it with meticulous care. Up at the crack of dawn, he gave himself a good all-around sponging. His feet needed more than a sponge, though. Making sure those heels were neat and good looking required a lot of rubbing with either a dried corncob or a coarse stone. Using both alternately, Phae scrubbed his heels and feet to the desired levels of cleanliness. By eight o'clock he was immaculate: bare but clean and vaselined feet, and nicely ironed khaki shorts and shirt. His face was clean, bright, and cheerful. After double-checking his appearance in the living room mirror, he found his way to the Bophelong "commercial" center and its lively newspaper peddlers, whom some preferred to call vendors.

This morning the established vendor Phae met was a tall, pot-bellied school dropout whom everybody called Willy. No one knew his real name, and no one knew for sure how come this kid came to be called Willy. Phae did not want to get embroiled in Willy's affairs, so he never asked personal questions of Willy, which Willy did not mind. Willy's world view was simple: in the beginning God created the world and all living things. Happy with the product, God decided to give man the seventh day to rest and read the newspapers. To the end that this latter objective could be achieved, God guided man to the formation of the CNA—the Central News Agency. Willy was the CNA's prime agent in Bophelong. Employed by the CNA, Willy belonged to the CNA soccer cheer group, owned a CNA delivery bicycle, wore the CNA uniform, and belonged, lock, stock, and barrel to the CNA gang.

His message was bawled across Bophelong's streets in loud staccato tones: "CNA! CNA! CNA! Here, please. The Bantu World! The Bantu World! Folks, here's the Johannesburg Bantu World! Golden City Post over here. This way to the Post!"

Occasionally, Willy would lower his sales pitch to "Ntate le 'me—dad and mom, come for your news! Over here is the Sunday Times of Johannesburg. Times! Times! Times, please!"

Phae, glad to see Willy, called out loud and clear, "Willy! Willy! Eh, come over here, man!" Willy turned to face Phae with his rotund tummy following in tandem. When their eyes met, there was a spontaneous outburst of delight.

Managing to push the bubble gum he was chewing into some hidden cavern of his palate, Willy declared, "Phae, man, I must see you this afternoon. Would that be okay by you? Please say yes; it's so important to me."

Phae must have nodded in agreement because Willy yelled, "Fantastic! I will be waiting for you next to the elementary school gate. By the way, do not forget the newspapers. Here they are. You can pay me later." With that, Willy tossed an assortment of local dailies onto Phae's lap before refocusing on the other prospective buyers.

Phae bundled up the papers and was soon on his way home. It gave him a peculiar satisfaction knowing Willy, a kid whose world was as unlike his as day differed from night. Willy was a member of the dreaded CNA underground, a highly organized, mobile, vicious, and pornography-riddled gang. His nights were spent at notorious hideouts and shebeens (speakeasies), where gang members had access to, among other things, illicit, white people's liquor. It was a world where matekoane—weed or ganja—was relished, and gang members boasted of the size of "bomb" they could roll and keep in place throughout the smoking session by licking it with doodles of saliva. It was a world of the super sensuous phata-phata dance—appealing, teasing, exotic, and dangerous. In Willy's world it couldn't be over emphasized that danger lurked everywhere, and it frequently exploded in gunfire or the flashing of three-star, six-inch knife blades.

How Willy functioned in this strangely fascinating and frightening world intrigued Phae. Willy was his contemporary, but an unpredictable twist of fortune and biology had given him a physique and visage that was both young and adult at the same time.

Robbed of the bliss of virginal youth's innocence, Willy sought to deprive what he thought was a malicious fate of its ultimate triumph by associating as frequently as possible with age-mates and ex-school mates. Observers, including Phae and his friends, recognized the immense possibilities for good and evil in associating with him.

To Phae there was nothing particularly "Bantu," "World," or "Bantu-Worldish" in the Bantu World publication that Willy used as his lead sales item. To Phae, the *Golden City Post*, the second lead sales item, was a purveyor of vulgar pornography and violence, and within minutes Phae had tossed the two aside. The liberal *Sunday Times* detained him longer, but none of its articles bore any relevance to him. Its comic section, however, was well done, and it had Phae laughing frequently. After reading the papers, it was time for dinner. Phae's mom, Lydia, or Ntlapu as everybody called her, made sure that everybody was punctual at the dinner table.

Sunday dinner was probably the week's most important meal. It was on Sundays, and Sundays only, that Phae could look forward to a full, three-course dinner. Soup was always served. It was homemade—nothing in Phae's family was ever bought precooked. Tonight's soup seemed to have been cooked from a combination of items from his father's butchery and vegetables from the local markets. The main course featured barbequed chicken, mashed potatoes, green beans, and a side plate of beet root steeped, to Phae's joy, in vinegar, and thick slices of raw onions. Dessert was classic—thick chunks of homemade preserved peaches adrift in thick, sweet peach syrup. Knowing the state and status of her menu, Ntlapu beamed angelic happiness. Short, liberally endowed, and possessed with an infectious sense of humor, she flitted between kitchen and dining room with admirable nonchalance.

Phae's father, Jeremiah, or Jerry as folks called him, was cast in a totally different mold. Born and bred in the ultraconservative Dutch Reform church traditions, he had a solemn and most awe-inspiring view of man's destiny in general and his in particular. To him, it was his divinely decreed duty to take his life and worship most seriously. For him, there was little time for frivolities on earth. Life to him was basically work and worship, with family somewhere in between.

When he was a farmer—and he had farmed all over the Vaal Triangle—work was farming to perfection. He had the best plows and the best oxen to do the job. He knew and practiced the most up-to-date farming techniques, from fertilizing soils with cow dung to making small dams for family and farm needs. Further, he was a genius at locating the key homestead site determinant—water sources—using a "y" shaped live willow branch to detect presence of underground water.

Beyond his farming-related accomplishments, Jerry had other skills that Phae could never figure out how he had acquired. He owned and played a piano, was excellent at watch and clock repairs, and, most surprisingly, was a brandy connoisseur par excellence who always graciously offered his guests a taste of the best. His interpersonal skills were probably his greatest asset and probably the key factor in his rapid rise to leadership in the Bophelong community in particular and the Vaal Triangle in general.

God had blessed Jerry with a decent-sized family: a beautiful and hard-working wife from the Evaton Tau family, eight kids—four boys and four girls, and an indeterminate number of family dependents. Jerry loved all his family members, however they had originated.

Jerry occasionally viewed Phae with mixed feelings. On the one hand, he was completely and absolutely pleased with the Lord almighty for giving him this son—a boy who was at the same time healthy, fit, dutiful, and above all, studious and obedient. This was a son, a gift from God, whom no father could underestimate in these trying times of mass departures from Holy Writ. By the same token, he knew the frailties of human nature and the ceaseless flow of temptations facing him. In the days of yore, hadn't God tested the strength of man's convictions in the aberrations of their offspring? Jerry was equally proud of his other sons, from the eldest, Ben, to those who came after—Phae, William, and, the last of the boys, Molupe (Modoopee).

Ben was Jerry's most-beloved son—even tradition dictated that. Ben was dedicated and hard-working and was currently on winter break from Marrian-Hill, a Catholic boarding school in Natal province. Jerry knew that the single most important determinant in Ben's life was his passionate concern for his father's stresses in managing his multifaceted business and community interests. Ben knew—and Jerry feared—that sooner than later he would have to give up academic pursuits and rescue his father.

Another concern that haunted Jerry was Ben's health. Ben had genetic and acquired frailties that were not improved by Ben's occasional usage of traditional cures. It was crystal clear: Ben's days at Marrian-Hill were numbered; family needs dictated that he, as the eldest boy, would have to give up academia to assist his father to rescue a business enterprise that was in sore need of modern management.

William was, of all Jerry and Lydia's children, the most enigmatic. Gifted with many social skills, William had succumbed to the temptations of marijuana and other street drug concoctions. Jerry and Ntlapu's fervent pleas for him to stop went unheeded.

Molupe, the last of the boys, was, like most last-born boys, his mom and dad's most beloved. In fact, everybody loved Molupe. He was at all times comfortable with all family members. Phae and Molupe were as close as any siblings could ever be. They shared many interests that were dynamic friendship makers: swimming, camping, and the analysis of contemporary developments in the print media. In Phae's view, Molupe was a genius in discovering people's—and Ben's in particular—hidden gifts. It was Molupe who discovered that Ben had a genius for teaching mathematics that neither Bophelong nor the local educational system could unlock—and at a time when mathematics teachers in South Africa were scarcer than gold. With the secrets of mathematics unlocked by Ben, Molupe could sail through medical school and end up marrying Gemmina, a beautiful registered nurse from northern Transvaal.

That day's dinner, for reasons Phae couldn't decipher, soon assumed an unusual characteristic: intimate, in-depth father-to-offspring discussions.

It began with a simple invitation. "Phae Phae, my son," his dad called out. Jerry preferred to use Phae Phae, the full nickname, rather than the abbreviated version, Phae. Phae Phae was a family nickname. Its origin was probably from the comic strips the family liked. Could it have something to do with Popeye the sailorman?

Gemmina, Molupe's wife, the "beautiful registered nurse from northern Transvaal."

Phae's grandfather called him by a different name: Senyaka-nyaka, the complex one. Still other family members called him Tseole—a name with intriguing historic associations.

However Phae Phae had originated, Jerry stuck to it. "Phae Phae," the old man continued pleadingly, "come and sit next to me after you finish your dinner."

Phae finished off the last teaspoon of the homemade peach preserves and deposited his used plates and silverware in the sink for washing before responding lovingly to his father.

"What is it, Dad?" Phae inquired, looking, uncharacteristically, straight into his father's eyes. For a split second their eyes met in utter silence. It was a pregnant silence. "No, Phae Phae, my son. It's nothing really serious or unusual. For starters, I just want you near me," Jerry answered, casting a blank stare into the outer heavens. "Lately, my son," he continued, "we have not shared much time together. And yet so much is happening to all of us."

Phae was taken aback. "No, no, Dad," he timidly responded, clearly surprised by the unusual revelation. "We have been together," he added defensively before he was half choked up by his father's candor. "Together," he mumbled before discovering he was dumbstruck. His father's statement was painfully and disturbingly true.

Old Jerry spoke softly, almost inaudibly, but with an unmistakable determination. "Today in church," he continued, "I made a promise to myself in the presence of God. From now on, I intend to spend more evenings at home. My wife, my sons, and my daughters deserve more quality time than I have so far given them. The school board, the Bophelong municipal advisory board, and the many other committees and subcommittees can function with my minimum participation. Tomorrow ..."

"Hey, what are you two carrying on like that for?" Phae's mother cut in. "I hope you are not giving poor Phae Phae the usual list of don'ts."

"Ntlapu, my dearest, it's nothing like that," Jerry answered, barely disturbed by Ntlapu's unexpected animated interruption.

"No, dear mother!" Phae added with suppressed enthusiasm. "Dad was saying he is going to spend more evenings at home."

"God bless my soul!" exclaimed Phae's mother. "What's that I heard you say?" she asked, determinedly.

"Yes, Mom, Dad's going to spend more time at home in the evenings," he replied, adding emphatically, "With us! Yes, with us only!" Phae's joy at this was exploding. The announcement from his dad had no precedent. Phae looked at his mother with joyous disbelief displayed prominently in his eyes.

"But Jerry, my dear, dear husband, how can you say that?" she asked in passionate surprise. "You're away from home evening hours, whether at the store, or church, or community affairs meetings. These things are your life. They are your daily feed. Your bodily system needs them. Your work is your life; it is you. You live off meetings and work. It's your staple," she concluded, tears streaming down her cheeks.

Noticing his mother's tears, Phae reached for a napkin to hand to her so that she could wipe the tears. Ntlapu appreciated that gesture. "This son of ours," she whispered to herself, "is a gentleman in the making."

"No! Ntlapu my dear wife," Jerry answered, adding timidly, "Meetings are not my work, nor my life. I go to meetings after my work hours," he tried to continue, but was forced to stop when Ntlapu decided to deliver the equivalent of a knockout punch.

"You don't understand me, Jerry, do you? Your work never stops at five o'clock or on Fridays. Your work is your total self; it's you. You and work are one entity. Meetings are nothing but an extension of your work world. Meetings and work is you, your total self," she concluded, signaling that it was time the conversation included other family members.

The other family members were, understandably, reluctant to join the discussion. There was Ben, the elder of the boys, on vacation from his Natal boarding school, seated at the far end of the dining table. He had too many study-related tasks to afford getting immersed in a family discussion that was exploring new frontiers.

Taciturn by nature, he announced, "I guess I have been gone for too long to connect with your concerns, Mom. I know how hard it is for Dad to have to run the store and be involved in all these community affairs. Sometimes I wish I didn't have to pursue further studies and could be home here, helping."

"No! No!" Jerry burst in. "You are not going to quit school just to help me turn my life around! No, Ben. School is far too important for you, for us, and for the future of our country. There is no way we are ever going to win the struggle against apartheid with you undereducated. Make no mistake about it, my son. As long as you want to study, I am going to give you my total support. And nothing, I repeat, nothing, is going to come between me and that goal." He paused, looked fixedly at Ben for a few seconds, and then, casting his eyes at others, he continued. "To all of you, I want you to hear this loud and clear. Your generation is going to change the course of this country. For generations we have let the Boers dominate us in the hope that God almighty would intervene. God has not intervened. And God will not intervene. It's up to us to continue the struggle against apartheid. And basic to the anti-apartheid struggle is education, the education of our youth. With our youth solidly educated, we will be able to overcome all the obstacles standing in our way toward being free citizens of a democratic, nonracial South Africa."

Phae was visibly moved. He had never heard his father talk like this. Phae felt something had changed his father. What could it be? And what did he mean when he said we have let the Boers dominate us? Did we let them dominate us while we placidly waited for God to intervene? This didn't quite square with what Phae had assumed were the facts. Didn't the black people of South Africa resist Boer domination throughout history? Could it be that their resistance was compromised? For the first time Phae had cause to doubt the quality of his ancestors contributions. Did our ancestors acquiesce in apartheid in the hope that God would do something about it? He felt like asking but did not know how to word the question.

"Dad," he managed to say. "Dad, could you please pause and explain. I feel lost and confused. I thought we were always taught to respect our ancestors and their traditions," he concluded nervously.

"Respect, my dear son, is respect. Not imitation. Not continuation. Respect in this context is simply an acknowledgment that our ancestors confronted situations as best as they knew how. Each confrontation in life has to be faced on the basis of its determinants. You do not go to the past to ask *'how did they do it?'* with a view of repeating it. You ask *'how did our ancestors do it?'* in the context of their times and their knowledge. Do not underestimate our ancestors' capacity for innovation. Whenever they could, they adopted new technologies, new strategies. How else do you think Moshoeshoe defeated the Boers when they tried to conquer Lesotho? He did not ask, 'How did my ancestors defend their territories?' He asked, 'How can we defeat an enemy equipped with firearms?' The answer, Phae Phae, was, 'Use up-to-date technologies.' In Moshoeshoe's context, it meant working with the French missionaries and acquiring modern firearms. Also, getting horses to give you flexibility in movement. But over and above these, it meant getting a primary defense resource that is sustainable and affordable. And what was that? Thaba Bosiu, a Lesotho mountain that was, until the invention of aerial bombardment, impenetrable and yet capable of accommodating and indefinitely sustaining the Basotho nation's armed forces. The Boers and their gods could never defeat the Basothos. If you keep the Moshoeshoe example in mind whenever you are asked about the advisability of doing things according to our ancestors, you will be on the right track.

"Another example of the same genre," he continued, "is to be found in Tshaka's, the king of the Zulus in the nineteenth century, revolutionary modernization of his armed forces. Among other things, he introduced the use of the metal shaft to the Zulu spears. The decision to use metal instead of wood was not based in tradition. Similarly, he realized that his times called for the emergence of nation states and not tribal kingdoms. He converted the several tribal groups in his part of the world into a powerful Zulu nation.

"For a nation to be significant, it has to be sustainable," Phae's father continued. "To be sustainable, the newly created Zulu nation needed effective, rapid deployment and well-trained armed forces. To maximize weapon effectiveness, Tshaka abolished the army's use of the long spear. Henceforth, the Zulu armed forces were to use short, effective spears. These were not to be thrown at enemies or beasts as was traditional. That was too wasteful. Efficiency and effectiveness required drastic changes in the ways spears were utilized. Henceforth, spear bearers were never to throw but to stab at close range. In implementing his innovations, Tshaka did not go to the ancestors to ask for guidance; he simply assembled the best advisors and used pragmatism to arrive at decisions.

"To all of you, my dear sons and daughters," Phae's father emphatically remarked, "I want to make this clear beyond doubt: the long-term interests of South Africa are in your hands." With education and continuous questioning, you can advance the agenda. Without education disaster and ongoing oppression and suffering is our fate," he concluded.

Phae stole a look at his mother. The blood vessels in her face and arms were sharply defined, a definite sign that this discussion had escalated beyond the norm. With that realization, Phae decided that discretion was the better part of valor and stole, with almost professional stealth, out of the dining room and out of the house.

With Phae out of the house, Jerry's compulsion for self-restraint was mitigated. Feeling completely exhausted by his presentation, he half rose and walked across the corridor separating the living room from the dining room toward the master bedroom. In the bedroom he stopped and looked at the bed the family had used since his marriage to Ntlapu in 1929—decades ago.

Since that unforgettable wedding day on the banks of the Vaal River, the family had existed by entering into all sorts of sharecropping agreements with local, white, farm-owning interests or individuals. Jerry's sons and daughters were never told even the basics of the agreements. From what Phae had observed, however, some basics were clear: his dad must have agreed to plant corn commercially on the farms and share his crop with the farm owner after the harvest. Since the heavy machinery required to thrash the corn commercially was either owned or rented by the white farm owner, the latter knew the exact number of bags harvested and collected his share the day that the corn thrashing was over. Jerry's musings in the bedroom went beyond recollections of past farming agreements to an uncomfortable confrontation with a question he had posed to the family earlier regarding his expressed wish to spend more evening hours at home.

As he lay on the bed, he realized that from now on he could no longer afford to let his desire to redeem his community be undertaken at the expense of his family. Furthermore, wasn't it time he started a life of normality instead? What, though, in his immediate geographic and historic setting, constituted normality? Is it normal for a black man to be a preacher in a Dutch Reformed Church where the white preacher's wife wouldn't shake a black woman's hand at a church located in a black neighborhood before putting on a glove? Was his membership in the Dutch Reformed Church contradictory to his profound belief that segregation was evil and had to be terminated?

From these musings, Jerry drew the one conclusion that was to radically alter his life: he decided to leave the Dutch Reformed Church and start a church of his own. Arriving at this stunning conclusion gave him an immediate peace of mind that was calming. And calmness is conducive to sleepiness. Within minutes, Jerry was sound asleep.

Ntlapu, noticing Jerry's status, kissed him gently on the forehead and whispered, "Sleep well, my dearest. We all love you."

With his father sound asleep, Phae remembered an appointment he had made. Yes, he had a late appointment with Willy. Within minutes, appropriately armed with a six-inch pocketknife, Phae was on his bike en route to Willy. Sure enough, Willy was waiting for him at the designated meeting place. Something about Willy told Phae that this was no ordinary meeting.

After the usual greeting Willy declared without further ado, "Look, Phae! I have discovered a way to make money quick and fast!"

Phae was stunned by the bold announcement. "Money?" he asked. "Hell, man, that was the last thing I was expecting you to talk about, he said," adding, more to himself than anybody else, "Money for what?"

"Money for what?" Willy fired back. "My gumboot! Don't be silly, man. Money for what, you ask. What happened to you? Look at yourself: no shoes, socks, or hat. No nothing. And you still ask, 'Money for what?'"

Phae was not shocked by Willy's insistent and vehement reaction. He was simply puzzled. Furthermore, a number of pieces did not fit together. First, Willy was a genius at selling CNA merchandise—there was no denying that. But whoever heard of Willy initiating and managing any money-making scheme successfully? It was known by all of Phae's friends that Willy had completely failed to be successful at selling oranges. Most kids would buy a bag of oranges from the farmer's market downtown for between eight and ten shillings and resell the same to the commuting public for a one hundred percent profit. If Willy made twenty-five percent profit he was lucky. A worse outcome had awaited his initiatives with apples and sweets. He ate all his profits before completing any sales, thanks, in part, to his accommodating tummy! Secondly, Willy disliked any projects with any elements of immediate personal danger unless they were associated with a high certainty of CNA black employee gang protection. This scheme didn't sound like it had the CNA gang backing, so what was Willy up to?

"Okay, Willy," Phae declared. "Come straight. What are you talking about?"

"Right!" Willy replied. "First, I trust you and you trust me, fine? Now, I am going to tell you all my plans, but if you don't want to come in with me, please do not tell any of the boys, okay?"

"Fine!" answered Phae, a little intrigued but otherwise maintaining an unexpected air of detachment.

"Now, let's get going. First, you know the big Boer-owned store in front of the police station?"

"Yes," Phae answered.

"Well, my scheme is simple. I have discovered an easy way to get in and out of the store at night without anyone noticing."

"Explain, please," Phae responded with benign amusement.

"The front of the store," Willy continued, "facing the police station, is always lit. The back of the store, however, is enclosed by a six-foot-high brick wall and is always dark. My plan is: we scale the wall, cut the locks holding the burglar bars on the windows on the back of the store, peel off the putty holding one of the window panes, and ply the pane out without breaking it. And bang! You have a wide-open entry into the store. One of us will have to go in while the other stays outside keeping an eye out for any intruders. Whoever goes inside collects the merchandise needed and, in no time, there you are—your money's made!" Willy's enthusiasm was obvious and palpable.

"That sounds too good to be true, Willy," Phae responded. "Just a little too easy. First, how do you know you can cut the locks?"

"Easy, I discovered that by accident. Last week I had made deliveries to the store through the back entrance as usual and was forced to wait for an unusually long time. I had in my hand a short piece of a metal saw blade. Being bored, I started testing if my metal saw could cut the lock, and in no time I noticed I had sawed more than halfway through the lock hook."

"God almighty!" Phae exclaimed, realizing for the first time the extent of Willy's emotional involvement in this scheme.

"Yes!" Willy responded enthusiastically. "That's what I said to myself—God almighty! How could the Boer store owner be so stupid?"

Phae couldn't have asked for a trickier situation. Here was a good pal of many years wrapped up in a scheme that could easily land him in prison for a few months or a youth reformatory for a few years. Admittedly, the scheme was feasible, and Willy could escape with the goods, money, or whatever was in the store that Willy thought would be convertible to cash, but it was a major criminal offense. There was no escaping that, not even the fact that a Boer owned the store. Two courses of action, then, seemed open to Phae. One, convince Willy of the dangers inherent in the plan or, two, give him a good lecture on the ethics involved in shop breaking and theft and the punishment in the hereafter, whether administered by the gods or the ancestors. Phae dismissed the ethics approach; leave that to the clergy and ancestor worshippers. He figured he had a better chance with the rational approach with an emphasis on the technicalities.

"Willy," Phae shouted hypocritically, "the scheme sounds

wonderful! Boy, you are great! I would never have figured out a way that easy to make money. Never!"

"Really?" Willy answered with an air of satisfaction and self-adulation.

"I say never!" Phae repeated. "But look, Willy, there are some things to clear up before you pull a job this big."

"Yes, but I can take care of that. Don't worry," Willy responded.

"First," Phae began, slowly and deliberately, "how do you know there's money in the store?"

"Of course there's money in the store," Willy fired back. "Folks use money to buy things, don't they?"

"Okay, but that doesn't mean the money stays in the store all the time," Phae answered.

"Oh! That figures!" Willy exclaimed. "Is that why they leave the cash registers open? When I first saw that, it didn't make much sense. But then, where does all the money go to?" Willy asked with unexpected earnestness.

"See, there's no need for the store owners to keep anything other than small change in the store. They make all their payments by cheques. So, whatever cash they collect from their customers finds its way soon to the bank," Phae concluded, hoping that would be one more negative nailed in the project that Willy would understand and appreciate. For a moment it seemed to have worked.

"Hell, Phae! I didn't know that, man. Is that the kind of stuff they teach you in school?" Willy replied.

"Yes and no," Phae replied, his confidence in the rational approach somewhat returning. "The next thing to keep in mind is this: If you can't find money in the store, your next best bet are the goods—shoes, pants, shirts, et cetera. Fine?"

"Yap," Willy replied with diminishing enthusiasm.

"Now, how do you fit your shoes in darkness? How do you choose the label or color or size? What do you think? Suppose you don't care about a size or color or label, you will end up with stuff you will have to sell, and that, I think, is one whole heap of a mess you don't want to get caught in, Willy. What do you think?"

Willy was not thinking. He had started walking away long before Phae could finish—head facing down, shoulders drooping, and his rotund tummy somehow deflated. Willy was a perfect image of disillusionment. Phae hoped it would take Willy more than CNA gang backing to resuscitate the scheme. He was wrong. His hopes were doomed.

Chapter 3

The winter school break was soon over. Lekoa Shandu High reopened with some dramatic announcements. Apparently, as a modification of the government's apartheid policy in general and "Bantu education" in particular, the successor to Vander Merwe was to be a black man. And guess what—not only was he black, but he was also a Fort Hare University baccalaureate with a postgraduate education diploma from the University of South Africa.

As the headmaster introduced him during the first post-school break assembly, he came forward with the brightest, most pleasant, most charming, most engaging smile the students had ever seen beam from that section of the assembly grounds. He stood tall, though he was a diminutive five feet six inches. His shoulders were thrown back. His hands, though, were still deep in the waistcoat of his black suit. Clearly young at heart, he must have steamed past his forties, Phae thought. It was clear to all and sundry, however, that Mr. Daniel Tambo, BA, UEd—a South African postgraduate teaching diploma—wasn't going to allow his age to be a factor in any of his educational pursuits.

Following Mr. Tambo's introduction, a program of school reorganization was announced. Its most important feature involved the introduction of some type of specialized teaching. Gone now were the days when a Vander Merwe could teach the seven subjects in the curriculum. A corollary of this was the need for a new timetable to allow either teacher or student a change of classrooms. A reactionary, retrogressive curricula objective was announced: From henceforth, school graduates were to be equipped only with that body of skills, knowledge, and attitudes that would "fit them to function within their own tribal groups." This announcement caused a ripple of giggles, escalating to unbelievable laughter and then swerving suddenly and threateningly to resentment and anger.

Under normal circumstances the principal would have started threatening the students with his cane for this unauthorized behavior. But there was nothing normal in this announcement, nor in his tone, nor in his reactions. Every fiber in his constitution had always rebelled against anything suggestive of tribalism. Now to be made an instrument of a devious policy was worse than any punishment he had to bear. To him now silent in the face of the students' reaction was not expedient. It was as imperative as it was a signal departure.

The first few weeks of the spring term were slightly confusing, and often upsetting, but never dull. Mr. Tambo, thank God, lived up to expectations! Moving with undeniable self-confidence from class to class, he infused history with a dynamism that had never before been seen nor thought possible in the Vaal Triangle.

Tambo saw history as a drama of the human story. It was the drama, among other things, of individuals passionately searching for and struggling to overcome perceived or real human and environmental obstacles to progress and improvement. History was also a multidimensional drama, a drama often involving passions, lust, and rapacity—a drama to subdue environments that were sometimes hostile and unredeemed. The drama of history was sometimes accompanied by shocking failures and atrocities, including exterminations of communities and other incredibly shocking acts such as genocides and enslavements. Failures and bloodsheds and Machiavellian intrigues have, however, in Tambo's view, never erased the thread of human triumph that has always weaved its way through the drama called human history. The critical era in the history of humanity in which all these forces were operational, in Tambo's view, was the French Revolution and the Napoleon era that followed. When presenting Napoleon, Tambo did not present facts; he acted out the drama right in front of the class. The thread that Tambo always sought and always dramatically illustrated in bold relief was the thread of triumph in the institutionalization of progress.

The joy of attending a history class taught by Tambo emanated from many sources, including new perceptions of human progress, where before Vander Merwe's lessons dwelled on facts and dates to be memorized and regurgitated during tests.

Soon it was spring! Oh, spring! There were moments of almost ethereal joy in being young and healthy in the midst of a South African spring. As if it happened all of a sudden, nature awakens from its winter slumber and explodes in gorgeous colors and sounds. Cycling or walking down to Bophelong from Vanderbijl Park, you could see peach and other trees in bloom stretched ahead of you for miles. And all over were birds of all colors and sounds darting hither and thither, blissfully welcoming the new season. Lawns, hedges, and flowers were all coming alive in the pleasantly warm, sunny spring.

The vigor and vitality of spring caught Phae in its embrace. But unfortunately, so did other less auspicious developments. On an innocent Thursday morning, Phae received a gift parcel from Willy. The wrapping was poor, but the contents were a veritable shocker: a brand-new automatic wristwatch and a Japanese camera. Phae was visibly shaken. He literally trembled with fright at the prospect of what could have happened—and worse, what this could imply. One thought struck him with lightning clarity and suddenness: Willy had broken into the store!

Yes, Willy had broken into the store with the help of three other boys. Everything had proceeded according to Willy's plan, and now, in celebration, he was distributing the largesse with careless abandon. For Phae, the occasion was excruciatingly painful—rejecting the gifts would amount to a rejection of Willy's faith, trust, and friendship. Acceptance was tempting but fraught with danger; how could poor Phae explain to anybody how he had come to possess these expensive items outside the Christmas season? Could he claim they were gifts from his Evaton relatives? No way. His Sharpeville schoolmates? Forget it! Were he to keep the goods, how long would it be before the police became involved? The police? Oh, hell! Yes, the police, especially the officers from the C.I.D.—the Criminal Investigation Department—and their notorious third-degree interrogation methods. Caught between the hammer and the anvil, Phae decided on an imperfect solution: bury the gifts in his compost heap until some as-of-now unknown force could yield an answer regarding what he should do.

As if propelled by an inexorable fate, Willy's shop breakings increased in daring and frequency, and with each operation Willy was undergoing a most fundamental transformation. The neighborhood's most popular newspaper vendor was now playing truant and, when in attendance, bawled with markedly decreased enthusiasm. Further, those who cared could not fail to notice the new external image of Willy: new multicolored shoes, new brand-name pants, shirts, and jackets, a stylish hat, and, unbelievably, a large, expensive wristwatch. Thick, stylish shades completed the picture. His new image was accompanied by an unfortunate but not completely unexpected style change in dealing with clients. He now had a faint but unmistakable conceit in his voice that was exacerbated by his tendency to order people around, where before he used to employ charming, friendly persuasion.

Phae could not relate to the new Willy. And it wasn't because Willy had turned to criminal ways—Phae had suspected that for some time. And it wasn't because Willy wore fancy new clothes and was cocky. No, Phae could not relate to Willy because he was now a dangerous boy— and particularly dangerous to those who had not embraced his new ways. Phae tested the venom of the new Willy one Sunday morning when out to purchase his morning papers.

"Willy! Willy!" Phae had called out, painfully trying to add warmth and normality to a voice torn by concern and fear. Willy pretended not to hear. Phae called out a second time closer to Willy.

Willy gave a little jerk, swung halfway around, and answered with unmistakable deliberateness, "Yes! Oh, it's you?"

"Yes, man!" Phae replied, concern gaining uncontrollable ascendancy in his tone.

"Ja! (Afrikaans for yes) You want your newspaper?" Willy asked acidly.

"Yes, but I also want to talk to you," Phae replied.

"Where's your watch? You didn't like it, yeh? And the camera? I have never seen you use it. Where are they?" Willy's voice was becoming more strident.

"That's my business," Phae replied with unexpected firmness. "I won't tell you or anybody else. Further, you won't see me use them tomorrow, next week, or maybe even next year. You see, Willy," Phae added with firmness, "I have my style and you have yours, fine? Let's keep the two separate."

Willy was taken aback by Phae's reaction and responded apologetically, "Easy, man, easy! You know I meant no harm."

"Better not have," Phae shot back, adding, " but for sure there are some things we better get straight."

Weeks later, Phae had cause to recall this conversation with startling clarity. For three days in succession, including a Sunday, Willy was not seen at his famous vendor's site. Word soon got around that plain-clothes policemen had been seen visiting his home. No one knew for certain what the policemen wanted, but the grapevine had it that a cohort of Willy's was shot during an attempted store break-in and was now a patient in the acute care section of the Vereeniging hospital—there were no hospitals catering to black people in either Bophelong or Vanderbijl Park. Most likely, Phae thought, the poor fellow was forced to "spill the beans," to use Willy's jargon.

On the fourth day following Willy's disappearance Phae noticed a grayish Volkswagen buggy parked outside the headmaster's office and two athletic-looking police escorting one of Willy's recent friends. It was obvious that somebody had given the juvenile thorough third-degree treatment.

Minutes later Phae was called to the headmaster's office, identified, and whisked off to the police station. The drive to the Vanderbijl Park police station was a nightmare. All types of horrors crowded Phae's imagination—the worst included visions of periods of indefinite imprisonment in cold, ugly, dirty cells infested with lice, fleas, and feces. Imprisonment would most likely be preceded by the administration of corporal punishment on his bare bottoms. "How did they do it? How?" he kept asking himself. Rumor had it that sometimes they did not use a cane but a whip made from hippo hide. Rumor had it that the end of the whip was five-pronged, and each prong was wrapped tightly with binding wire. For greater cutting effectiveness against black bottoms, rumor further had it, the hippo-hide whip was stored submerged in salt water. How was he going to be held down on the bench? Ropes? Additional police? Should he bawl or should he accept it sullenly? Before the whipping, what degree of force was used to obtain confessions? How was this applied?

Phae's face turned ashen upon seeing Willy. It was a shock with an otherworldly aura about it, midway between the shock suffered by Adam when he first laid eyes upon Eve in paradise and that of Caesar upon seeing Brutus's murderous dagger. He staggered, stumbled forward, and crash-landed on a wooden bench, gasping for air and reassurance.

Neither the most outrageous fiction nor the weirdest tales of prison torture could have prepared him for a sight so incredibly revolting. He tried to crawl out of the place, disappear, run away, or vanish from the face of the earth! Seeing the policeman's black boots, however, wiped the thought away. Screaming seemed to be an alternative—yes, a viable one. He took a deep breath, opened his mouth in one desperate, defiant gesture, but nothing came out. Not a sound, not a whimper, only a choking, inexorable sense of doom. He struggled to get up, first on all fours, next with his hands on the bench, and then up the dull gray walls where his sweaty palms failed to produce the faintest imprint. At last, achieving a type of erect posture, he turned, took a long look at Willy, and fell forward in one thunderous messy heap. Upon recovery, Phae was ordered to return home on one condition: not to discuss the details of this visit with anyone.

Phae never found out who or what killed Willy. Rumor had it that elements of the Vanderbijl Park CNA gang inflicted the initial punishment and some drunken Afrikaner police and their Alsatian dogs finished the job. However it had happened. Willy's mutilated frame was never seen. The efficient police apparatus took care of all body disposal details.

Chapter 4

As spring merged imperceptibly into summer, Bophelong's surrounding landscape changed its hue. Fruit trees, mostly peaches, shed their flowers' bright petals as well as their seminudity and began to assume a sober, dignified greenness as their young leaves sprouted. Wild bird life—real or perceived—lost its early spring vitality, freshness, and appeal. Birds began to be seen not as objects of beauty but as destructive pests that followed farmer's plows searching for the corn seeds that farmers wanted left alone to be covered by the first rains. Domestic stocks, recovering from the starvation days of winter and early spring, began to show a healthy luster in their glossy furs. Cattle began to clothe their erstwhile exposed ribs, thanks to greater access to soft juicy spring grasses, as they started adding pounds. Cattle weight gain had an unwelcome aspect for the herdboys: cattle began to move with assertive arrogance and stubbornness that often forced the herdboys to cuss with revealing furtiveness as they desperately drove their herds away from young corn plants.

Summer in South Africa is pregnant with expectations for the young. There is, first and foremost, the promise, if not certainty, of a warm, sunny, and colorful, joy-filled Christmas. And Christmas was the only time of the year when a black kid could expect—with a high degree of certainty—to receive, unconditionally, gifts from parents and relatives. And the gifts would, invariably, be primarily clothing. While Christmas clothing gifts were valued for their long-term usability, what the kids loved most on Christmas Day itself were items that all households gave away in abundance: homemade cakes and juices.

Throughout Christmas Day all households would have their doors wide open for walk-in visitors asking for Christmas gifts. Each visitor, dressed in all manner of weird, Halloween-like outfits, would announce at the door: "Merry Christmas!" The response from the hosts would be equally loud and cheerful: "Merry Christmas to you! Here's your Christmas cake and juice."

Adults would frequently be offered home-brewed beer. Some would respectfully say, "no, thanks," but most would down the brew. The effects of too much Christmas beer consumption would, invariably, soon show. To many, the beauty of South Africa's traditional Christmas observations derived from a different source: the colorful beauty of freshly redecorated traditional homesteads.

Almost exclusively, the women of the household did the redecoration of the homesteads. They crisscrossed the land in search of appropriate earth colors for decorating the walls. They collected fresh cow dung to use for decorating the inside floors. They decided on the beautiful patterns and intricate but fluid artful designs that were the outstanding characteristics of the culture. When decorating the walls, the women did not use brushes—they used their broad palms to spread the mixtures. The use of palms assured symmetry as well as designs both geometric and intriguing if not unfathomable in their expression of a people's craving for creativity.

Where concrete structures such as those that characterized Bophelong's households precluded creative, palm-spread expressions on outside walls, people resorted to ordinary, brush-on, commercially available paints for interiors. It is important to know that whatever media was used and whatever barriers were encountered, nothing could dim these people's spontaneous bursts of self-expression. Creativity flowed out with a forceful gentleness and tenderness that more than once sent tears streaming down Phae's unabashed cheeks.

Phae knew with certainty that his palm would never reproduce the forms and shapes that flowed so naturally from the women's hands. Unashamedly unable to help the women with creative redecoration,

Phae enjoyed the one field in which his talents commanded a respectable mastery: the construction of food and beverage preparation facilities.

Cakes were the single most important Christmas food item to be prepared. And for their preparation, the bottom-line most important item was a stove. You cannot have baked cakes without a stove with an oven. So, come Christmastime, if you did not have a stove with a baking oven you had to construct one—no ifs, ands, or buts about it. Phae's family this Christmas season did not have a stove with a functional oven. It was a mini crisis to the family. To Phae, it was a godsend. Unable to help with creative decorations, Phae rejoiced in the one Christmas-related field in which he commanded respectable expertise.

No doubt about it, ovens could be made in various ways. The most practical way, Phae thought, was rooted in tradition: the conversion of anthills into baking ovens. To construct an oven this way, your first chore was finding, ideally, a dead or ancient anthill. Once an anthill of sufficient size and structural soundness had been located, it was dug out of its moorings and the inside was hollowed to the required shape and size. Once this stage was completed, a smoke hole was punctured in the back and an oven door opening carved out in front. The oven door could be any left over metal scrap; for example, an old shovel blade that was no longer strong enough for digging or similar purposes. In under an hour, an anthill finder could have, pronto, an oven with excellent heat retention capabilities. And it was in search of an anthill that Phae took off on this clear, bright, and beautiful summer Saturday. Pickaxe and trowel in hand, he leaped over the garden mesh-wire fence, whistling on his way to the open veld.

South of Bophelong the land slopes gradually toward a micro-dam and a lethargic spring. A significant landmark separated these from Bophelong—a major dirt road with a cluster of Indian-owned stores located on both extremes. The micro-dam that Phae's father had constructed and the lethargic spring supplying it with water was bounded by what appeared to Phae to be ancient, lightning-torn, gigantic weeping willows. Phae knew that the moist lands surrounding the dam and spring were unlikely to have anthills, alive or dead. This notwithstanding, the lands had an irresistible fascination for Phae. It was a fascination rooted in facts both mediate and immediate.

Phae's father had personally engineered and constructed the dam while he had been a sharecropper on the farm of a white family that used to own this side of Vanderbijl Park and Bophelong. To scoop the earth out of the area designated for the dam, he initially used a deep-cutting, ox-drawn plow to loosen the earth and followed this with a similarly ox-drawn dredger shaped like the top of a wheelbarrow to scoop the dirt out of the projected water-storing dam. Phae's older brother had watched the operation with boyish fascination. Now, years later, it was amazing how, silting notwithstanding, the dam had defied time and now stood, isolated and almost unwanted, as a lonely landmark visited only by young lovers and adventure seekers.

Two things about the dam fascinated Phae immediately. First, there was the possibility of a nude swim. Secondly, the vicarious sexual excitement of catching, unseen, lovers romancing on the cool, soft, natural lawns that were common along the willowed stream. Whistling and singing in careless abandon, he reached the dam wall with only his mariner briefs guarding his decency. Seconds later, his briefs were gone and it was in splendid nudity that Phae dove into the shallow but familiar waters. The cold chilliness of early summer open waters sent refreshing shivers throughout his system. Phae adored the sensation. To him it was the "it" of swimming.

Diving under, Phae was almost gentle with the waters, afraid that too much splashing might stir the layers of dirty mud underneath. Easing himself between broad-leafed lily plants, he swung sharply, turned over, and lay prostrate on top of the waters with the sun warming his belly and genitals.

It was almost an hour later when Phae emerged from his angelic repose. Dreamily refreshed, he wandered back into the veld in search of an anthill. He frequently had to stop to pull out an annoying thorn from his bare feet or negotiate a difficult path between thorny weeds. It was during one of these unpredictable stops that he caught sight of them.

From a distance he could have sworn he had seen the man before. There was something uncommonly familiar in his labored gait and his short, heavy-set frame. He could not make out the girl who was behind the man and therefore half-hidden by the man's frame. Something about her, though, gave Phae the feeling that she was young, slim, and pretty.

Aware that the couple had not seen him, Phae hid in the thickets while keeping his eyes excitedly fixed on all of their movements.

Their conversation was, initially, too subdued for him to hear at that distance, but the frequent bouts of laughter and giggles told him that it was a ticklish and erogenous conversation. Yards from him they stopped. All the conversation and laughter also came to a halt as they embraced each other affectionately. Phae could see the man's hand stroking the woman's waist and gently but surely moving up to her bosom, neck, and ears. Intermittently, the man embraced her breasts and moved his hands rapidly down to disappear under her skirt.

Responding to his caresses, she flung herself into his arms, rested her face against his chest, and slowly started caressing him with feelings of passionate tenderness. Her long, slim fingers worked around his neck, back, bottom, and disappeared somewhere where Phae guessed his zipper should have been. The first time this happened, Phae saw the man's movements come to a sudden stop and slowly resumed as the woman worked her way up. The third time she did it, Phae saw the man stop and clutch the woman tightly, as if responding to this. Her hands now lingered longer in the zipper region. Phae's eyes were now boyishly wide open. He could barely resist the temptation to stand and swallow the delight of the entire scene. Against the profoundly tense silence of the afternoon, Phae's heart beat with a sledgehammer effect against his chest. He was never so engrossed, nor so fearful. The love scene was now unfolding with dramatic spasms. Before his enthralled eyes, he saw the man's pants crease, cling to his thighs, and slowly fall below his knees. Phae knew that was her doing. He saw it written all over her triumphant face as she turned to look around to see if somebody was nearby.

For what seemed like an eternity nothing happened, and then, suddenly, a heart-tearing cry tore through the afternoon air: "Elizabeth! Elizabeth!! Oh, Liz! No! No! No!" It was so loud, so clear, that Phae trembled. For a split second he suspected foul play. What could the woman have done to the man? What? Should he rush out to the man's rescue? Would the woman recognize him later? What if she were to attack him? "God, what an awful mess I'm in," he thought, looking for the one weapon he knew nature provided in abundance: stones. There were none in sight. None, fortunately, were needed.

Phae saw the man lift up his arms, kick out his left foot, and then cry out in one dramatic gesture, "Liz, Liz, I love you. I love you, Liz. But please, honey, don't do it again. I beg you."

He tried to hold on to her but staggered back and fell, tripped by his own pants. For the first time Phae had a full view of the woman's triumphant, almost mocking, but undoubtedly expectant face. Brown-skinned with big, black eyes and lips hidden by a thick smear of lipstick, she pulsated in desire. This time there were no whispers. Phae heard her clearly. "I'm coming to you, dear Joe, baby. I'm coming, baby!"

"It's too late", the man replied faintly.

"No, dear, it's not too late," she assured him. "This is just the beginning. Remember what you promised? Once the tension is over you had said we could take our time. Remember those words? I am coming baby. I want you today. Yes! And right now!" And with that, she flung her wrap-around skirt wide open and dove onto poor Joe.

With the two half-hidden by the thicket, Phae slithered away like a reptile until he was clearly beyond hearing distance of the two lovers. His sense of relief was astonishing. He had never been that dangerously close to people making love, nor had his emotions been that wrapped up in an illicit scene before. Away from the lovers he sighed heavily and sat down to recover. Several minutes later, having regained his composure, he scampered for his tools. As soon as he found them, it was back to the original mission: the search for the anthill.

It was not until late in the evening that thorn-pricked, emotionally wrecked Phae found a desirable anthill. Located in the shadows of an aged, ribbed, thorny acacia, the anthill was bald and denuded, with no ants in sight. It was indisputably dead, and an indisputably dead anthill was what Phae was looking for. This anthill was a gem for oven purposes. With sunset eminent, all Phae could do was to stake out his claim by making rudimentary, peripheral diggings around the anthill to indicate that the anthill had been claimed. To easily identify the spot from a distance, he attached a newspaper leaf on the outstretched branch of the acacia. Having done this, Phae hurried home, vaguely wondering how poor Joe hoped to fulfill his promises. Furthermore, he thought, it seemed odd that the two were still at it this late.

After supper Phae made an unusual decision—to walk to Bophelong's commercial center this late and after all the day's excitement. One factor tilted the decision. It was a beautiful, starry, cool, and invigorating night. Phae walked out through the living room, thereby avoiding having to explain to his mother, who was in the kitchen area—you could exit the house through the kitchen door—why he was going out. He locked the door behind him and pocketed the house key. At the gate he paused, admired the healthy poplar tree he had planted in front of the courtyard, and momentarily surveyed the cul-de-sac that was Nhlapo Court. He looked at the sight in front of him and reminisced about the days when he thought he would make the cul-de-sac a landscaped beauty. In the midst of reminiscing, he remembered a crucial detail—he was not equipped to handle trouble. He hesitated and then decided he would enjoy the outing better if he were prepared for trouble. He decided to return to the house to pick up his trusted defensive and offensive weapon: his five-star, six-inch blade knife. With it secure in his back pocket he walked out with briskness and determination.

On the way to the shopping center, he stopped by to see his old friend, Richard, alias "Foozy," and started recounting his unauthorized glimpse of Joe and Elizabeth's amorous encounter. Richard was enthralled and decided to join Phae on his walk.

Some Bophelong streets were wide, well lit, and edged by shade trees. The streets also boasted fairly adequate pedestrian pavements. At night, however, most people avoided the poorly lit pavements and stuck to the main roads. Fortunately, vehicular traffic was limited. Bophelong boasted only one licensed taxi. There were probably no more than a dozen cars among all the residents—with only a fraction of those being operable at any given time. The center of Bophelong was a simple square. On its northern fringes were stores in strip-mall formation.

Phae's dad owned a deli-restaurant combination in the strip mall called, "The Bantu Café." He also owned a butchery outlet adjacent to the store. Attached to the butchery was an Afrikaner-owned store with what Phae considered expensive merchandise. Behind the butchery and store was the bus terminus. On the east side of the square were several small stalls selling a mixture of consumer products. Phae's closest friend for years, Philemon Ndlozi Radebe, used to run one of these, but after his father's death he had to relocate to Tsirela, on the other side of Vanderbijl Park, to manage his father's larger grocery store.

The southern fringe of the square boasted Bophelong's one and only community hall. It was in this hall that Phae fought his way to local fame in amateur boxing. It was in this hall also that he saw most of his early teen movies. He could recall some of the heroes of these with ease: Gene Autry, Roy Rogers, and the Durango Kid were his favorites. Next to the hall were the post office and the local municipal offices. On the west side of the square but across the street was Bophelong's only medical health-care facility—a clinic that was staffed by nursing aides.

The middle of the square, which showed signs of failed landscaping attempts, was an empty lot bustling with men, women, and children. This small crowd was often turned on by popular musical hits blasting from a nearby outlet. On weekends when some of the crowd had had a little too much of the local beer, music-churned excitement reached levels pregnant with possibilities—frequently frightful possibilities.

The Jeremiah Tsolo legacy

When Phae and Richard approached the square, they noticed a disturbance at the entrance to the Bantu Café. Soon they saw the crowd inside rushing for the doors in panic. Panic degenerated into total confusion. Phae and Richard knew that anytime a Bophelong weekend crowd became chaotic, disaster loomed. Fights were likely to break out between individuals and a gang or, though rare, one gang against another. Fights were Bophelong's most dependable and exciting weekend attraction. However, when fights spilled over from being individual encounters to gang warfare, they ceased to be entertaining and became veritable hell-fire wagons of destruction.

The cause of tonight's fight was never clear. Speedy rumor had it that a local sleek—Tsotsi, some would call him—had pickpocketed a Poqo tribesman out of his weekly earnings. The tribesman must have spotted the culprit. With machete and knob-kerri waving menacingly, he chased after the miscreant. The thick crowd around the square slowed down the pickpocket's escape. This enabled the tribesman to corner him outside the fruits and vegetables market. Sensing victory, the Poqo man came in for the kill. With escape routes shut, the youngster resorted to reason. "Mdala! [Old Man] Please stop it! Why are you chasing me? Why?"

"Why? Why, you ask!" he replied. "You little devil! I am going to kill you! Where's my money?" The Poqo man was steaming with fury.

"What money are you talking about? Hey, Mdala, there must be a mistake. What money?" the youngster insisted.

"Give me back my money!" the tribesman responded with a note of finality.

Richard could not take standing out of the bristling confrontation anymore. He knew the youngster to be a rotten one. But he also knew the youngster had done a few people good turns that had been financed with jewelry stolen from white folks. Richard somewhat suddenly remembered that he himself had been, in fact, a personal beneficiary of this youngster's criminal exploits in the form of an expensive wristwatch. Having followed the machete-edge interlocution, he took a cue from the boy's bag of tricks and was heard to holler above the expectant crowd's din: "Mdala, here's your money!"

The mdala swung in the direction of Richard's voice. That gave the pickpocket a split-second opportunity to make his getaway. In a flash, his shadow scurried into the bowels of the night.

The break of dawn found Phae up and busy in the yard, preparing a resting place for his anthill oven. Soon after sunrise he went back to the veld and on to the path leading to his chosen anthill. The anthill was easy to locate, and in no time Phae was digging away around the edges of the anthill to make sure that he would tear the structure from its moorings with minimal damage. It was no easy task. The earth was stone-hard clay. And worse, the anthill rested on a hidden crystalloid boulder. With patience and accurate strokes, however, Phae unmoored the anthill before midday and was ready to start the journey back home when an irresistible thought intruded: why not revisit the site where Elizabeth and Joe had had their amorous affair the other day? Why not? Phae couldn't resist. He yielded to the impulse.

As Phae started toward the spot his expectations were vague; only an irresistible temptation urged him on. Carefully avoiding thorny scrub and bush, he made his way to the spot with a hunter's instincts. Nothing stirred in the scrubs below him, but when he looked above him at the clear sky he saw the plateau's notorious scavenger vulture, in majestic solitude, hovering above the area. It was an ominous signal. Just yards from where he thought he had last seen the lovers, he was forced to an abrupt stop by a scene he saw with unforgiving anguish, hatred, and fear. There it lay, coiled in one lethal heap, a deadly adder, overfed from a previous kill.

He circled the lethargic but colorful killer in widening circles hoping to sight a stick or stone with which to attack the snake. In spite of exercising extreme care, he still accidentally stepped on something unusual; it was soft, bulky, and not organically related to the surrounds. He was forced to stagger in confusion. The soft bulk was the half-nude body of the male lover, swollen to twice its original size. The nude girl lay just a few feet away, dead, with her mouth wide open.

On closer inspection, Phae noticed puncture marks on her neck and chin. They showed some signs of bleeding. It was a scene at once ghastly, repulsive, and remorseful. Phae gave a one ear-splitting cry and ran. And ran.

He tore across bush and savannah scrub, cleared dongas and ancient rock outcroppings, leaped over hedges and fences, and outpaced nervous, noisy mongrels until, with toes bleeding and sweat pouring from every pore of his black body, he collapsed in front of Municipal Police Inspector Japie Malan.

Japie Malan was a tall, red bull-necked, thoroughbred Afrikaner from the Orange Free State province of South Africa. Life had taught Japie two unforgettable lessons: one, the wisdom of having administrations of Bantu locations manned by Afrikaners who were God's appointees and anointed; and second, the absolute necessity of keeping the black kaffirs in their rightful place. These lessons were, to him, sacrosanct.

Turning his scornful eyes on the collapsed bundle that was Phae, he mouthed, "Hey! Hey! You bloody kaffir! Move your blasted ass off that carpet."

"Yes, yes, mister!" Phae managed to faintly reply.

"Yes, what?" Japie glared. Phae acknowledged his mistake and answered in the apartheid-endorsed manner. "Yes, baas (boss in Afrikaans)."

"You damned kaffirs are bloody cheeky," Japie fired back. "The next time you mister me, I am going to kick your balls out of here!"

Phae, struggling to regain his breath, knew what comments to ignore.

"Nou, wat soek jy (Now, what do you want? in Afrikaans), boy?" Japie asked, happy he didn't have to use his boot on Phae.

"Dead!" Phae replied nonplused. "Dead! They are dead!" he added.

"Jesus Christ, you bloody rude kaffir. What are you talking about?" Japie yelled in fury, half-suspecting that the dead might be white, in which case hell was going to break loose. Realizing this, Japie leaped from his comfortable office chair and roared over Phae: "Praat [talk] kaffir! Praat before I knock your damned teeth out! Who are they? Are they white?"

"They are dead," Phae answered, flat as a pancake, all fear drained out of his system. Looking straight and fearlessly at Japie, he warned, "Please, do not ever call the Lord's name disrespectfully. If you do, you and yours will be doomed." Japie pretended not to have heard while simultaneously suppressing the instinct to give Phae a good plodding kick in the ribs.

Instead, he opted for persuasion. "Tell baas who they are and all will be all right," he said. "Who are they?"

"Dead," was Phae's flat response.

"Jesus Christ!" Japie exclaimed. "You Bantus are hopeless." Opening the door to an adjacent office, he yelled, "John! John! Kom hier nou, nou! (Come here now, now!)." Any black policeman under his command was a John to Japie. In answer, a John appeared to get the information from Phae that Japie had attempted to solicit so unsuccessfully.

Chapter 5

There are rivers whose names recall all types of romantic legends and daredevil adventures; rivers whose attributes have fired the imaginations of men and led to immortal works of art. A perverse fate had denied this to the Vaal. Yes, when the Dutch Voortrekkers crossed it, they called the territory beyond the river Transvaal—lands across the Vaal—but what romance lies in that? Nor even in Boer mythology do you find a poem dedicated to the Vaal River. To the Africans, the name of the river was and will always be Lekoa. It was dull, muddy, and often tepid, and at times furiously overflowed and threatened bordering settlements. Whether dull or furious, the Lekoa River, in local mythology, buried mysteries in its wake. Beneath its often-lethargic surface, local African mythology goes, lurk man-eating monsters of legendary dimensions, including horse-headed reptiles known to change abodes following cyclonic disturbances that were accompanied by tree-burning lightning and thunderous explosions. These fearsome monsters were not strangers to kindness; stories were told of lost strangers who were given overnight lodgings in the monsters' underwater dwellings.

To Phae's crowd, the history and mythology of the Vaal was irrelevant. As far as they were concerned, the Vaal was the biggest known accessible concentration of dynamic water available for miles around. Because of its size, strong undercurrents, and wooded banks, it had an unequaled romantic and adventurous appeal for people of all income levels, colors, and ages. It also, unfortunately, had its nonlegendary dangers. On its shores the dividing lines between blacks and whites were tragically undefined and shifty, established often by priority in arrival. It was the, "I got here first today, and therefore I am the exclusive owner of this site for today" mentality. If priority in arrival was not convenient to use, the next leverage resorted to was old-fashioned brutal force. If blacks did not accept the claims of the Afrikaner to the swimming site, then it was God's order that they be made to accept that by force, which was made more potent by the certainty that if the police were to arrive they would, without question, enforce what they deemed were the rights of the Afrikaner.

When plans for what became Bophelong were drawn, the Calvinistic Boer planners must have had some good intentions, but whatever good intentions they had, these did not include constructing swimming pools for the initial fifty thousand residents. Consequently for the Bophelong residents in general and Phae's friends in particular, if you wanted to swim, you did so either at the Vaal or the shallow, silted dam that Phae's father had bequeathed to posterity. Naturally, in allure, the Vaal, despite its dangers and accessibility obstacles for Phae's friends, won hands down.

The Vaal was approximately fewer than ten miles south of Bophelong. Access to it was easy for the privileged. For starters, a modern superhighway linking Johannesburg and its sprawling suburbs with the new town of Sasolburg—Africa's only coal-to-oil fuel production city—passed within a stone throw of Bophelong's police-guarded entrance. Clearly, the privileged could simply hop into their sedans and in minutes be basking on the banks of the Vaal. Neither Phae nor any of his friends had family members who owned a car—regardless of its condition. The closest to a vehicle Phae's gang could claim were three bicycles. Quite clearly, a trip to the Vaal for Phae and his friends was a relatively major undertaking necessitating carefulness in planning and execution.

Among the problems to be overcome in organizing a trip to the Vaal were, first, transportation. How do you move a dozen boys over this distance when you have only three bicycles? Cabs, buses, and trains were nonexistent on this route. What about hiking? Hiking as an option was out of the question. In the Transvaal some estimates suggested that ninety-nine percent of the motorized traffic was owned or controlled by hands unlikely to swerve to avoid striking a black hitchhiker on the roads.

The gang's solution to the transportation dilemma was ingenious: each bike would be used to carry four people. The main controls will be in the hands of whoever sat on the regular bike seat. The second rider would sit on the main frame at an angle. The third rider would sit on the handlebars with his legs resting on the axle of the front wheel. The fourth sat on the regular rear wheel seat. Whoever occupied the rear seat had the misfortune of having to carry most of the bulky stuff. Why? The rear seat was legal, solid, and dependable. In case of a misfortune, the rear-seat occupant had the greater likelihood of emerging either unhurt or with minimum damage to himself or the goods he was carrying.

Lunch posed a less intractable problem, but a problem nevertheless. Between Bophelong and the Vaal there were no retail outlets catering to blacks. All the food and water Phae's friends were going to need had to be hauled over that distance in one way or another. The improvisations the gang came up with were numerous: all of their pants pockets were stuffed with nonbreakable items, including fruits. It's surprising how many peaches a dozen boys' pants pockets could accommodate! Peaches were chosen with care given this mode of transportation—they couldn't be too ripe. Those that were too ripe would get crushed easily. The insides of shirts provided ample storage space for soft and bulky foods. Phae's shirt, for example, hid two loaves of whole wheat bread. For the shirts to be nearly reliable food storage areas, they had to be tucked well under the extra-tight belts in their short pants.

Defense weaponry often provided Phae's friends with their most complicated problem. No one in Phae's cluster of friends welcomed fights over swimming areas. Most emphatically did not want to engage in combat with anyone over so-called swimming rights. Unfortunately for them, though, fights over swimming areas were an ugly inevitability. In preparation for this, what were Phae's friends to do? Carry knives? No, that would be too dangerous. If any of Phae's gang were to stab an Afrikaner boy, their fate would be sealed—they would be hunted for eternity. Sticks or knobkerries? These required skills in short supply among Phae's friends. Worse, neither Phae nor any one in his group thought these to be appropriate. Basothos were good at these, but none of Phae's gang showed a stomach for that sort of thing. Worse, fighting with sticks required close combat with the high chance of being caught. Stones were more viable and plentiful. You could throw them with your bare hands, or you could use your sling.

Finally, with pockets stuffed with fruits and shirts bulging heavily with brown loaves of whole wheat bread—because of a scarcity of wheat, blacks periodically were not allowed to buy white bread—Phae and his crew shot out of Bophelong toward the Vaal River, using whatever shortcuts—usually meandering pedestrian dirt paths—they could find. It was not until after midday that they descended noisily upon the Vaal, settling finally in the shade of a huge, heavy, fire-gorged weeping willow. Seconds after settling, they were scrambling to the banks for a dive into the waters.

"Here I come!" shouted Samuel Mokete Mosiea, a flyweight amateur boxer and the youngest of the group, as he dove into the river. He hit the waters with a noisy splash. The others laughed loudly as they quickly jumped out of their clothes. In no time their small section of the river was one noisy, cheerful display of nudity and amateur swimming. After an improvised lunch, the gang exhibited varying levels of tiredness, and the Vaal seemed eager to accommodate them. Without anyone giving any signal, gang members spontaneously drifted to places where they could take a short, quick nap. They were soon sprawled in watery splendor under the willows. In almost idyllic heavenly repose, the gang seemed blissfully unaware of the passage of time.

It was the impetuous Samuel—the gang called him Sam—who decided to crack the silence descending on the gang. "Boy, it's hard to believe," he pronounced, addressing no one in particular.

"What?" two members of the gang responded spontaneously.

"Yes, it's hard to believe," Sam ruminated absentmindedly.

"Forget him!" screamed Phae as he swung to a lower branch of the weeping willow. "He's dreaming," Phae concluded. From somewhere below the branch Phae was comforting himself on, a member of the gang gave a deep cough and grunt as his contribution to the discussion and quietly turned over to sleep.

The usually patient Richard took a sweeping look at the array of seminude bodies and discarded lunch remnants and declared, "Boy! Hey, Sam, if you want to be heard, you better talk now. Soon the Afrikaner boys will be here and all hell will break loose."

Quietly philosophical, Sam turned to Richard. "Rich!" he called out. "It's hard to believe the end of the year and the final examinations are so near."

Before Richard could answer Sam, a voice from the riverbank yelled, "Damn you! Damn you all! Can't you talk about something else? Afrikaner boys and exams, Afrikaner boys and exams all the time. I am sick and tired of it. I came here to have fun, and by Kuena (a reference to his lineage; a Kuena is a crocodile in Sesotho), I am going to have it!"

The bellicose response came from Nyakane, a rough-hewn new arrival from Lesotho. His knowledge and fluency in Sesotho, the language of the Basotho people of the proudly British Commonwealth protectorate of Basotholand in the heart of South Africa, was envied by all. The difference between his Sesotho and that spoken by Phae's friends reflected the diverse impact upon South African blacks that the influences of detribalization, urbanization, and, above all, the cumulative impact of the Afrikaans and English languages had had upon them. Phae's Sesotho was a hybrid. In the presence of this Lesotho firebrand, Phae was sharply aware of the differences and knew, with some shame, that there was nothing that could be done by anyone to reverse the situation. If Verwoerd had shared Phae's convictions on this, South Africa's political evolution would have taken a different path, some would say.

"Okay, Nyakane! Take it easy, man," Phae interjected.

"I knew the Basothos were intemperate, but you are quite some Mosotho (the singular for Basothos)," Richard cautioned.

"You better all know," retorted Nyakane, with an air of finality, "a Mosotho is a Mosotho because of his Sothoness. And nowhere does that include fear of or obsession with either exams or Afrikaners." With that, Nyakane strutted away toward the river, obviously readying himself for a dive. But something stopped him suddenly. With his hands shading his eyes against the sun, he fixed his gaze on a moving spot upstream. Half-believing what he saw, he called out loudly, "Phae! Phae! Come here quickly!"

Phae and the boys leaped toward him, seconds too late! Nyakane had dived into the river and was swimming furiously toward midstream. It was Phae who first realized what Nyakane was doing. He heard the cry from midstream for help. The cry told him the identity of the supplicant—an Afrikaner, most likely a boy. Phae saw the youngster disappear under the waters as Nyakane's hands reached out to catch him. Nyakane must have caught the youngster because soon the boys saw Nyakane, in carefully measured strokes, slowly pulling the limpid victim to safety. It was an operation remarkable for its smoothness and precision. Almost miraculously, Nyakane knew what to do. No one knew how the rescue news rapidly reached the whites along the banks of the river. They were soon all over the rescue area. Nyakane seemed unaware of the peripheral developments. His attention was focused exclusively on the victim. His first step was the implementation of a classic rescue technique: assure that the victim was still breathing and making sure breathing passages were clear. That meticulous attention to detail proved tragic in this case. A heavy, tall, police-type Afrikaner, unable to stand the sight of black hands on a white body, kicked Nyakane on his right ear side with a viciousness that surprised everybody watching.

Nyakane rolled over once, apparently unconscious, with blood spurting from his mouth, nose, and ears. The stunned crowd rolled back and, for what appeared to be an eternity, no one moved. When the "whites-only" ambulance arrived, the drowning victim must have been dead. By a barbarous legislative enactment, neither the ambulance driver nor his emergency rescue-trained teammate could give Nyakane a helping hand. It was a sad bunch of boys who carried Nyakane on their bikes to the nearest "non-whites only" clinic—almost ten miles away in Bophelong.

Nyakane's recovery was slow—and never complete. His right eardrum was permanently burst and a spherical area around his ear was left permanently depressed—a lasting and unforgettable tribute to the viciousness of the kick administered by an undoubtedly devoted follower of South Africa's brand of Calvinism. With a split eardrum and a depressed right ear, Nyakane was physically and mentally altered.

Gone was the uninhibited spontaneity that had led Nyakane to several Wordsworthian, though unremembered, acts of kindness and love. These were replaced gradually but inexorably by a crafty Machiavellianism bent on revenge. It was a frightening transformation—even to those in Phae's circle who were thought to be hardened "toughies."

Nyakane's transformation was infectious. Phae's cluster of friends—a loose, fun-seeking but study-conscious bunch—was fundamentally altered. From being a fun-loving bunch of boys who occasionally engaged in minor scrapes with their white mates, the boys evolved into a gang and started taking the first steps toward a path of violence and bloodshed against anything supportive of Boer dominance. The transformation, imperceptible as a process, was indisputable in its short-term outcomes. Meetings became regular, organized, and planned. Attendance, hitherto haphazard, was now limited to a select core and was monitored. Loose, unstructured, and informal conversations were replaced by goal-directed discussions. Picnics as subjects of discussion were replaced by talks on incendiary bomb techniques, the acquisition of firearms, and, most ominously, inviting guest speakers to address the gang on developments in the current black struggles for freedom.

They acquired their first tool for a concrete "struggle for freedom," a firearm, almost by accident. A gang member's elder brother had forgotten his "Baby Brown" inside an overcoat that a gang member wore to one of the gang's meetings. Needless to say, the elder brother never again saw either the gun with its loaded magazine or the nearly full ammunition container that was never too far from the "Baby Brown."

Nyakane acquired the gang's next firearm, a German-made precision machine. This was stolen from the bedroom of a middle-aged Boer couple after Nyakane was forced to slit the throat of their Alsatian thoroughbred. He gained entry to the bedroom by smashing a window pane after carefully plastering its entire surface with masking tape. Subsequent firearm acquisitions were incredibly easy and splendidly illegal in a country where no black man, to Phae's knowledge, was ever allowed to possess a firearm regardless of justifying circumstances. Ironically, these subsequent acquisitions were facilitated by, among other things, a movement among white adolescents most portentous for the history of black-white relationships.

The movement originated, as did so many fashions of the time, from overseas, most likely in Britain. It was variously called the hippie movement or the duck-tails. Whatever the name, its adherents were unmistakable: they defied norms in their appearance, dress, language, and, most significantly, attitudes toward "matekoane"—ganja, dagga, weed, cannabis, or pot depending on your orientation or background. South African hippies cut across white racial divides: they included Afrikaners, English descendants of the 1820 British settlers, and other diverse European immigrants.

Of utmost significance to Phae and his friends was one characteristic of the hippies: they were not racists. They supported anyone, regardless of race or creed, who accepted their lifestyle. They were one-hundred-percent-dependable allies of anyone who facilitated their access to their beloved marijuana. For Phae and his gang, the unconditional acceptance of the hippies was almost a foregone conclusion in the post-Nyakane disfigurement era. It was in the white hippies' search for weed that they met Nyakane and Richard. The black youths' objectives were clear: ganja in exchange for guns and ammunition, or no deal. The hippies accepted this arrangement, and a crucial clandestine relationship was forged.

Possession of firearms was a far cry from mastering shooting techniques. It proved almost impossible to create conditions where the gang members could have anywhere near adequate target practice facilities. The denuded plateau of the Transvaal and the Vaal Triangle in particular was too open, and too vulnerable to penetration by police informers, to encourage any clandestine shooting practice. Scattered clusters of forest were too thin and too discontinuous to be viable. The problems associated with target practice were compounded by the nonavailability of near-expert target shooting instructors. The possibility of remedying this seemed remote in the early 1950s. Realizing the realistic limitations of the resources of the Vaal Triangle in black Bophelong's anti-apartheid crusade, Phae committed himself deeper into pursuing the one anti-apartheid weapon he knew had the highest likelihood of success—education and studying. This commitment yielded benefits with amazing rapidity.

Chapter 6

Probably the most exciting news for Phae during the 1956 Christmas season was the announcement that he had passed his secondary-school examinations with distinctions in all subject areas, including Afrikaans. Reports from those who were in positions to know suggested that his average scores were above ninety percent—the second highest in the history of the school, second only to those scored by Isaac Thapedi, the boxer from Sharpeville, a few years earlier. With that achievement solidly in his pocket, Phae set his eyes on his next target: matriculation. This meant applying to the Kilnerton Training Institution in the Pretoria area—one of the few matriculation-level boarding schools for black aspirants in the Transvaal province—for admission and, most importantly, scholarship. He got both with a rapidity and smoothness that amazed not only him but also his parents and neighbors, and, above all, his friends.

The one friend Phae felt bad about was his best mate from his elementary school days, Philemon Ndlozi Radebe. Not only was Philemon a close friend, but the two were academic fanatics and loved studying and scoring high on all tests and exams. After a family misfortune—his father's unexpected death—Philemon took over the management of his father's grocery and general merchandise retail outlets in Tsirela, and reports suggested that his business skills and innovations were unmatched. Philemon's move was also a loss to Phae in a different context: he had once been Phae's best tennis playmate. The two were smooth, self-taught players who used to practice on Bophelong's clay courts adjacent to the soccer fields. The congratulations card from Philemon for Phae's impressive secondary school certificate examinations performance was simple and touching. It read: "Remember the quote from Tshaka: "With God on your side, the sky is the limit!" Funny, Phae thought after reading the card; Vander Merwe, his junior-high Afrikaner history teacher, never knew that!

Not surprisingly, the beginning of 1957 found Phae boarding the train at the Vereeniging station en route to Kilnerton via Pretoria. His ticket was second class in the non-whites section. He had two suitcases with him: one loaded with his clothing and the other with provisions, not only for the overnight trip but with enough to ease him into his new life for months to come. You see, Kilnerton meals were well-cooked but never spiced—and Phae had a Caribbean palate when it came to food and spices. The overnight trip was tense. Phae had to be on guard. Why? The train had too many suspicious characters. To Phae, all strangers in unfamiliar settings were suspicious. Fortunately, no one challenged his space during the entire trip. Upon arrival at the train station servicing Kilnerton, there was a school bus waiting to transport arriving students to the main campus. And it was during this short bus trip that Phae met a boy from Sharpeville who, unwittingly, cast a huge, benevolent shadow in his new life.

The boy, nicknamed Stiles, began the relationship with an innocent observation directed at Phae. "Hi!" he said. "Are those real knuckles on your right hand?"

Phae was caught off guard. He looked at Stiles, uncertain how to respond, and stretched out both hands for Stiles to see.

"Hell, boy!" Stiles burst out loudly and clearly. "You are a boxer! Where are you from?"

"Bophelong, Vanderbijl Park. Next big town to us is Vereeniging. Do you know where that is?" Phae asked.

"Do I know where that is?" Stiles replied. "How could I not? I am from Sharpeville. Know what? It's great you are from our area. Now you are going to be in our dormitory. Welcome to Kilnerton home, boy!"

"Thank you! Oh, thank you!" replied Phae with excitement in his voice. To be called a "home boy" was the greatest accolade anyone could bestow on him at this stage. Further, to be a "home boy" had many connotations of immediate value: existence of a solid body of age-mates committed to his well-being in its totality, instant respect from all those who held the group of "home boys" in high esteem, and, above all else, easier access to dates.

Many must have heard Phae's conversation with Stiles. The first sign of this was the increasing numbers looking his way on the bus; some, in fact, had their eyes glued on him. From nowhere in particular, Phae heard the whisper, "He's a boxer. Be careful with him!" When he heard that whisper, Phae suddenly realized that he had a new status in this community. Unbeknownst to him at that early stage of boarding school life, his new status was going to exempt him from some of the humiliating, "Welcome-to-Kilnerton" secret hazing ceremonies. In this part of the world it was deemed to be extremely unwise to mess with a boxer with Phae's rock-hard knuckles—the product of years of swinging at the sand-filled punching bags in the gym.

Kilnerton marked Phae's transition from the Bophelong culture matrix and its bloodstained limitations to a new life full of the excitement and possibilities that only boarding schools of the era—apartheid notwithstanding—could provide. Phae's first significant move after arriving was choosing a dorm. The choice was, as Stiles had indicated, preordained. He was assigned to the Vereeniging area students' dorm. Few developments could have pleased Phae as much as this placement did. Sharpeville and Vereeniging were familiar to him. After all, he had cycled through them to get to Lekoa Shandu High for two years. But more than this, being assigned to a Vereeniging/Vaal Triangle area dorm meant that henceforth he would be living with a crowd of boxing lovers who inevitably would enhance his boxing skills. And he was not disappointed. Within weeks, the campus was abuzz with the news that a new kid from Bophelong was the most hopeful prospect for winning the Northern Transvaal amateur boxing flyweight championship.

Not only did Kilnerton enhance Phae's boxing possibilities, but it did something of more lasting significance: it taught him the more refined social skills that were missing from his semirural Bophelong upbringing. And of the social skills, interactions with girls were given top priority by the seniors in the dorm. A tall, teaching major and soccer player from Sharpeville, nicknamed Oupa, was, by a process that Phae couldn't decipher, assigned this task. Oupa went about it with the intensity of an American professional basketball coach's fanatical obsession with details.

The lessons covered the entire high school social interactions dynamics field, including how to introduce yourself to a girl you are hoping to go out with, how to invite her to an outing, what items to have with you on your first outing, and how to introduce these to the girl. The lessons included theoretical outlines as well as hands-on illustrations that were delivered with a candor and honesty that was remarkable for the age group. All participants were encouraged to use what they had learned in any and all encounters with girls and to report back to the dorm. It took Phae weeks to be comfortable with this aspect of dorm life. However, when he finally met the girl of his choice—Nancy Tau—everything changed as he found himself applying dorm social interaction theory with the precision of a professional and the steady determination of his ancestry.

Nancy, from the western Transvaal, an area Phae knew little about, was enrolled in the teacher training program and was in her second year of training. Phae thought that she was beauty incarnate, with a singing voice that dazzled audiences at local concerts. That she was willing to go out with him, Phae thought, was the outcome of some divine intervention. To show appreciation to divinity for facilitating this relationship, Phae found himself saying soft prayers at night, thanking the divine and the ancestors. Incredible as it might seem, Nancy was equally thankful and showed this in myriad ways, as she understood, more than any girl Phae ever met, that he hungered for true love.

High school love connections.
Top, Elizabeth Ngee Khosana. Bottom left, Phae. Bottom right, Nancy Tau.

Kilnerton's weekend recreational planners had a tradition of accommodating those who thirsted for love and romance. They were called, in local jargon, "Romanos." During picnic and camping outings, special arrangements were made for the Romanos regarding busing and romantic sites at destinations. And the lover boys were expected to provide themselves and their partners with appropriate romance-enhancement treats! Is it any wonder then that Phae, for years thereafter, viewed his Kilnerton days as fundamentally transforming? The haunting horror of apartheid in all its guises was significantly absent on the Kilnerton campus. The staff was evenly mixed, with one-third being black South Africans, and all others being comparatively recent professional recruits from Europe, especially the British Isles. Thus staffed, Kilnerton boasted an activist liberalism that permeated most aspects of campus life. Students had a wide choice of activities to participate in, from boxing to soccer to tennis and everything in between, including debating teams to jazz and hosts of singing and performing arts groups.

Brand new to Phae, at Kilnerton, students were not only expected but also enabled and empowered by the administration to participate in defining and implementing school policy by a simple mechanism: all organized student groups were required to send two representatives to Kilnerton's board of directors meetings. The students' representatives were entitled to vote on all issues on an equal footing with the teaching staff. Phae joined the board as a representative of the Debates Society in his second year.

Student attire in all these settings was formal; for the boys, it was a blue blazer, white shirt with tie, and gray pants. While the color of shoes was never, as far as Phae could remember, spelled out, to Phae the color of the clothing predetermined the color of the shoes—black. Phae, with an inborn conservative streak, loved the school colors and wore them without feeling pressured to do so on all applicable occasions.

For all of its praiseworthy positives, Kilnerton was not heaven on earth. It still bristled occasionally with tense situations. For years after Kilnerton, Phae had cause to remember one of these. It happened during an English composition class and bore some resemblances to an incident with Vander Merwe.

The teacher was an English expatriate named Eccles. Eccles was, beyond doubt, not a Vander Merwe and arguably not a racist. Eccles had asked the class to write a composition with the subject matter confined to a building they deemed impressive or outstanding. Phae, with minimum hesitation, chose the Kilnerton chapel atop the hill on the northern border of the campus. The structure was a classic Tudor—solid stone construction with a tower and a church bell. Phae loved the building, especially when seen from the bottom of the valley silhouetted against the blue South African sky. To him, it looked majestic and awe-inspiring, and his essay was a fluid, colorful reflection of this. On the day Mr. Eccles returned the student essay exercise books, he kept back Phae's. After all the exercise books were handed out, he tersely told the class, "There is one essay I would like to read to you. Please listen carefully!"

The class listened in complete silence. Silence, however, did not hide the fact that the class was impressed by the gusto and colorfulness of Phae's prose. It was awash in descriptive adjectives. After reading the essay the teacher did something most unexpected and shocking. He stood in the middle of the classroom with his face reddening in anger and yelled: "You seem to approve of this essay, do you? You should not. This essay is full of nothing but bombastic nonsense!"

Eccles marched with determination toward where Phae was seated and, in a move that stunned the class, he threw the exercise book at Phae while sermonizing. "Why do I think it is full of bombastic nonsense? Why?" the teacher asked the class. Without waiting for the class to respond, the teacher continued. "Because it furnishes no details about the chapel's structure," he concluded, clearly thinking he had made a convincing case against the essay.

Phae was stunned by the teacher's overreaction but did not take long before responding with uncharacteristic firmness, "Sorry, Sir. I beg to differ. Mine was a creative writer's perspective. It was meant to evoke emotional reactions from its readers. The emotional in your reaction is what I had hoped to tap. Had I targeted building-construction readers—whom I don't unashamedly know—my approach and tone would have been different."

Phae was surprised by his own reaction and feared, intuitively, that he might have come dangerously close to crossing the line. The class loved the encounter and soon suppressed giggles sent ripples of suppressed laughter among the classmates. The impending classroom chaos was terminated suddenly, but benevolently, by the lunch break bells.

Beyond the campus, the Kilnerton years exposed Phae to Pretoria, one of South Africa's historic cities. He soon found himself in love with the place and its cultural life. For the first time in his life, Phae could now see first-release movies at reputable but indisputably "non-Europeans only" cinemas. For the first time in his life, he found that he could walk the downtown streets without fear.

Two views of the famous Union Buildings, Pretoria

Somehow, South Africa's administrative capital had managed to be less stressed by the exigencies of apartheid. With decreased cross-cultural stresses came reductions in incidents of bloodshed and terror, whether from street gangs or overenthusiastic law enforcement agents.

Even nature seemed more approving of Pretoria. With a warm subtropical climate, its streets were lined with massive jacaranda trees that seemed to always be in bloom. Probably an area of Pretoria that Phae loved unabashedly were the Union Buildings. These were complex architectural wonders boasting the best-kept grounds Phae had ever seen. And it was during an incredible romantic moment on these grounds that he issued a momentous invitation to Nancy.

"Dear Nancy, would you please visit with my mom and dad during the next school holidays?" Phae pleaded, looking his beloved straight in the eyes. Nancy looked at him with her tender, irresistible, love-infused eyes that Phae adored and said, "I would love to, dear."

In that crucial, unrehearsed moment both knew intuitively that they were about to cross new boundaries in their amorous relationship with this invitation. Once Phae's family accepted Nancy, all of the hurdles to an engagement and marriage would be technically and traditionally cleared.

Issuing the invitation for Nancy to visit Bophelong reminded Phae of one of the few shortcomings Kilnerton posed for him: Kilnerton meals were lousy! All dinner meals were beans cooked and served without any additives to make them tasty. If you wanted to make them tasty, then it was incumbent upon you to provide the spices and whatever other additives you preferred. All Kilnerton did for you was to boil the beans to a pulpy, bland tenderness. Phae had been adequately forewarned about this Kilnerton shortcoming—hence the provisions in the second suitcase he had with him upon arrival at Kilnerton.

With Nancy having indicated a willingness to visit with Phae's family during the next school holidays, Phae immediately set the wheels in motion. He wrote a letter to his father introducing Nancy and informing him and the family that he would like her to visit with them during the next Christmas holidays. He was simultaneously tense and excited during the writing of the letter, but once it was completed he wasted no time in getting it mailed. Once this task was accomplished, he centered his attention on Kilnerton's other activities:

debates, boxing and gym, worship on Sundays in the local chapel, school-board meetings, and, above all, fervent studying.

Consistent with his elementary school days' promise, Phae took studying seriously. His study schedule was tight and faithfully adhered to: a minimum of two hours of study in the evenings, followed by work on homework assignments. His dorm-mates understood and respected his schedule, especially as this accommodated the social orientation "lectures" by the dorm's leading citizen and teacher training senior—Oupa, a name with an unmistakable Dutch/Afrikaner origin that literally means "grandpa."

When Oupa heard of the new developments in Phae's life, he decided to fast-forward his social interaction sessions to cover a field rarely visited—preparing Phae's dorm-mates for the inevitable in their lives, marriage. Oupa deemed it fundamental that the boys be well grounded in what he called "IWI: Intimacy Without Intercourse." No one in the dorm knew the origin of the concept, but to Oupa it was an emotion-filled driving force. Oupa would tell the group that intimacy between two people in love is a given.

"Without intimacy there cannot be love—not as we know and understand it," he said. "Can there be love without sexual intercourse? Absolutely yes! Our traditions required that before we could be married and licensed to have sexual intercourse with our beloved, we should have attended what is today erroneously called a circumcision school. These schools, in our forefathers' times, were not primarily for circumcision. They were created to instill adolescents with the necessary skills needed to be effective, caring, and loving husbands and wives. Circumcision was done as a necessary hygienic measure. The uncircumcised penis has an incredible capacity—as do so many of our body's excretion points—to hide and generate infections. We are not circumcised. We were never given detailed instructions by our parents regarding sexuality and related issues. Why? Because we come from supposedly modern urban locations freed from traditional encumbrances such as the educational opportunities offered by traditional transition to adulthood schools.

"I strongly recommend to you all the following: First, be faithful to those you love. Second, be intimate without sexual intercourse until you have been adequately prepared and your relationship has been sanctioned by whatever formal authorizing persons, organizations, et cetera that exist in your family.

"Third, remember that intimacy does not preclude touching and caressing each other's intimate parts; it simply precludes penal penetration."

"Fourth and finally, never forget that the consequences of penal penetration before marriage are too dire. They could include toppling the careers you are trying so hard to train for. And worse, you can end up with a range of infections that I am not equipped to talk to you about."

When Oupa ended his presentation there was complete silence, broken only by a reminder from a dorm-mate that it was now study time.

Phae still loved studying outdoors alone, especially on the slopes of the hill with the chapel forming its crown. On those slopes he could read aloud to himself while memorizing long tracts from his anthology. Frequently, Phae would find an unfamiliar plant or insect. Whatever unusual plant or insect he found was submitted excitedly to the biology teacher—a white, English lady who never failed to show fascination with his discoveries.

A Kilnerton experience that Phae found not only exciting but also eye-opening to the other side of South Africa that he had only read about was an encounter with an authentic South African member of traditional royalty in a nontraditional setting; there was a male student on campus who was a genuine prince. He was in the direct line of succession. Most importantly, his father, a current western Transvaal chief, was affluent. His territory had vast mineral deposits with mines yielding valued minerals and tax revenues for his tribe. Every other month, a convoy of stretch limos would show up on campus to visit the prince. Each time Phae saw the convoy drive past the dorms, he compared what he saw with the status quo in Bophelong; this convoy had more cars than were owned by all the residents of Bophelong!

Phae spent the last quarter of 1958 in a self-generated, intensive program of preparation for the university entrance examinations. These examinations, organized, monitored, and certified by the Joint Matriculation Board, were South Africa's most feared single examination. Students preparing for these examinations were quite often complete and utter nervous wrecks by the time the examinations were over. Quite frequently, a good number were casualties even weeks before the examinations, with a not insignificant number ending up in one sort or another of the country's miserable detention centers for persons with severe mental health problems. To those, however, who survived the rigorous study and examination pace, the governmental and commercial superstructures promised and yielded abundant returns.

The pressure on Phae to perform ironically was less severe than was possibly the case with candidates coming from older and more established urban areas where the full implications of a pass or failure on the finals were appreciated To the typical Bophelong resident, Phae had long outstripped their perceptions of what constituted academic success parameters. Most, if not all, understood what failure or success meant in elementary school. A lot understood the need to go to junior high. Once beyond junior high, the picture became fuzzy.

Relieved of pressures from home, Phae's pressures were self-generated. In fact, from his point of view, they were not pressures at all. Phae had an incredibly fixed but reality-based notion regarding his ability to pass the exams. He had absolutely no doubt of the outcome. What was questionable to him was the degree of excellence he would achieve in passing the exams. As long as the examination questions were derived from the prescribed study texts, his success was guaranteed. Why? His study habits were solid and had been so from elementary school days.

In elementary school he was always either number one or number two in excellence in his class periodic tests. When he was not number one, his best friend, Philemon Ndlozi Radebe, was. The differences in their scores were invariably statistically insignificant. Philemon was not there now; the death of his father had forced him to leave school and go into the merchandise retail world. But his presence was always felt by Phae, who had promised never to let any other student take Philemon's position vis-à-vis him when it came to examination outcomes—the statistical differences between his scores and the next should never be insignificant. And there was only one way he could make sure that incredibly lofty goal could be achieved: constant study and fitness, period. This was the operational side of the promise he made in elementary school after seeing the school principal whip a child for failing to do his homework.

Convinced of a successful performance in the Joint Matriculation Board university entrance examinations, Phae spent a considerable amount of time planning for the post-high school years, especially his secret goal: qualifying for admission to the highly reputed, nonsegregated Catholic university across the borders in Nyakane's homeland, Lesotho. Phae knew he lacked one preadmission requirement—membership in a Catholic church. With time indisputably limited to remedy this shortcoming, Phae focused his attention on this clear, achievable goal.

Phae's knowledge of the Catholics was extremely limited—confined largely to either the roles Catholics played in Mr. Tambo's history presentations or his occasional glimpses of nuns and priests, either in documentaries or as distant, strange, aloof, God-fearing residents of monasteries. Though little known to him, there was a strong belief among South African blacks that Catholic schools in general and the Catholic University College of Pius XII, Roma, Lesotho, in particular, provided the best color-blind graduate and post-graduate educational opportunities throughout southern Africa.

Phae began his quest for admission to Pius XII the only way he knew how: by careful planning with a meticulous attention to detail. His first obstacle was obvious: the nearest Catholic church was two train stations away in the Bophelong-like "Bantu location" of Mamelodi. What was the solution? Obviously, to generate enough income to pay the train fare and have enough change left over to make contributions during worship.

How do you generate income at Kilnerton? It was dicey but not insurmountable. The income-generating option he settled for was not completely out of character—photography! Something told him that his roommates and classmates would love seeing pictures of themselves in the many colorful settings that Kilnerton provided. The next step was to buy a camera and photo-processing equipment. But how was he to buy these items without cash? The answer was simple enough: generate cash to buy the equipment. How? Deny himself movies and luxuries for months to save enough. He even did weekend gardening jobs for local civil servants!

Before long, he bought an affordable but dependable Kodak camera and photo-processing gear, and in no time he was an accomplished and sought-after part-time photographer, generating enough revenue to buy the two-way Sunday train ticket to Mamelodi with enough left over to cover the inevitable contributions to the church as well as to fund dating and other "luxury" activities.

Phae's attendances at the Mamelodi Catholic church had several characteristics. First, punctuality. He was invariably on time for the first worship session. Second, participation in activities and discussions. Third, enthusiasm. Phae's enthusiasm was not fake; it was genuine. By understanding Catholicism, amongst other things, he might understand his father's frustrations with the Dutch Reformed Church. Fourth, appropriateness and respect. Phae was always dressed appropriately for Catholic worship. Fortunately, his Kilnerton school uniform was perfect for worship—it pleased the white expatriate clergy while conforming to Kilnerton's requirement: school uniforms during outings. What a money saver!

With predictable inevitability, the Mamelodi priesthood started noticing—and liking—Phae. And with undeterred single-mindedness, Phae made sure that not only was he noticed but that the priests knew him. To become known, he chose a means that he was most comfortable with—frequently asking questions on aspects of the church that he was either unfamiliar or uncomfortable with. During sessions of questioning from the priests, Phae would be at his angelic best. "Reverend and blessed father," he began on one occasion, "I have a burning need to know and to understand the nature of sin. I have talked to many people, both at home and at Kilnerton, but none of their explanations satisfy me."

"Yes, my dear son," the reverend priest answered. "I am glad the Holy Ghost has led you to our church and to truth. And now, please sit down and let me hear your problem."

Phae set down as the priest had requested. His seating position would be as recommended by his former Boy Scoutmaster: head straight up, shoulders thrown back, and chest jutting out. All the time, his eyes would be fixed inscrutably on the Irish, white-robed priest.

"Father," Phae began, "if all the things that we know to exist were created by an all-loving God, how do we explain the existence of evil?

How could an all-loving God create something evil? Something sinful and harmful and painful? Please explain, Reverend Father."

"My son," the white-robed, bald-headed figure answered, "it is obvious that God is working in you. Come, hold my hand, and let's walk together in the courtyard."

Holding tight to the holy hand, Phae made sure that an important detail was not forgotten. "Father, do you still remember my name?" he asked.

The reverend father paused, looked at him, and declared, "Yes, my son. Your grandfather was born in Lesotho and migrated to South Africa before the turn of the century to work, some think, in the Johannesburg gold mines. He came from an ancient cattle-farming stock with West African roots who were thought to have arrived in southern Africa at least one hundred thousand years ago. The initial West African stock loved living along the coast where edibles were easily accessible. His ancestry includes a man who point-blank refused to give the Afrikaner soldiers his horse for combat during the Anglo-Boer war. When he wouldn't surrender his horse, the Afrikaner decapitated him and threw his head into a shallow stream in the Orange Free State province. Your grandfather's stint at the mines was short. Soon he was back into farming; that is where your father, Jeremiah, acquired his farming skills. Your father is, by all reports, a great man. We hear about his efforts to help the people of Bophelong in several areas. His ceaseless efforts to prod the government into erecting more and better schools for the people of Bophelong and the surrounding Vaal communities have not gone unnoticed. We support him, even though we are unable to explain his loyalty to the Dutch Reformed Church."

Phae was stunned by the priest's knowledge of his history. How did he know all of that? For the first time, Phae thought he had been outsmarted; the priest must have done his homework. If what the priest had said so far was surprising, the following stunning revelation shook Phae to his core.

"When your father married your mother, Lydia Ntlapu Tau, in 1929, expectations were great," the priest continued. "To everybody's surprise, your father constantly delivered. He met and exceeded the expectations of the sharecropper deals he made with white farmers in the Vaal areas even during the World War II years."

"Father!" Phae exclaimed. "Please stop. How do you know this?" he asked, with anxiety and concern written prominently all over his face.

"Donald," the priest answered, resorting to unexpected formality and looking Phae straight in the face, "whatever information we have on those who worship with us is acquired the only way we know how: prayer and research. When you showed by your worship and attendance a seriousness of purpose, we did what you always do so well—researched our subject."

Phae was highly impressed. If this Mamelodi priest could acquire so much information about him and show so much thoroughness in his research, what did this suggest about Pius XII University College? His zeal to gain admission to that Lesotho Catholic university college increased greatly.

"Thanks a lot, Reverend Father," Phae managed to say. "I am glad and surprised that you know so much about my history. I am truly impressed. Coming back to this question of evil ..." Phae couldn't complete his sentence because he heard the priest continuing: "It's sad, isn't it? There you have in Jeremiah a man who is strong, upright, and in good health. A self-educated, staunch member of the school board and the Bophelong municipal advisory council," the priest went on, oblivious to Phae's efforts to speak. "How do you explain that?" the priest concluded.

"Explain what?" Phae responded, half-exasperated.

"Jerry had opportunities for conversion better than others, but what happened? He clung to the Dutch Reformed Church with an incredible and almost incomprehensible tenacity." The soliloquy was transforming him from a man to a voice as his age began to assume a divinity that momentarily scared Phae.

"Father! Father!" Phae pleaded, trying to bring the priest back to concrete reality.

"Can you see me? Can you hear me? Please, Father."

"Yes, son, but can you see and hear your Father?" The multifaceted question caught Phae completely off guard. He reeled back in astonishment.

"Father, what do you mean?" he asked.

"I mean nothing other than what your heavenly Father intended, that you hearken unto no other but that which comes from Him and is witnessed in Holy Writ and the traditions and customs of the Holy Church."

"I see," murmured Phae, confusion written prominently over his furrowed brow.

"If you can see it," the Holy Father answered, "you are blessed!" And with that, he turned and waved good-bye to Phae who stood perplexed and fearful that an expedient stance might have unwittingly led him to a confrontation with unknown supernatural forces.

The information packet with the admissions application forms from the University College of Pius XII, Roma, Lesotho, arrived within two weeks after Phae posted the college-entry application letter. The forms were surprisingly simple and asked mostly routine questions, but there was one vital question Phae had to answer. On the application form, it simply asked, "Indicate religious affiliation, if applicable."

Phae knew that his response to this simple question could be decisive in determining his acceptance. With self-conscious, defiant boldness, he filled in, "Catholic." Further, where the form requested references, Phae had the audacity to name the priest! He also, of all things, went personally to the priest to request from him a letter of recommendation! The priest, after some initial reluctance, agreed. Within two weeks, Phae received the admission letter, which was valid for the next two years.

Receiving the admission letter from Pius XII University College was probably Phae's happiest moment. He jumped, ran, cried, and laughed his way from the post office to the dormitory. Negotiating the last obstacle before reaching the dorm, he stopped, looked at the bright-blue Pretoria-area sky and thanked God from the bottom of his heart.

Somehow in that blissful moment, he knew a forgiving and caring God existed somewhere! On the weekend following the good news, Phae bought two two-way train tickets to Vereeniging—the nearest train station to Bophelong. One ticket was for himself and the other was for Nancy. Upon their arrival in Bophelong, he found, to his surprise, that the good news had been blasted far and wide with the rapidity of a winter veld fire fanned by the ghastly southeasterly winds.

On the night of his arrival, they came from all corners of Bophelong—young and old, friends and foes, in all sizes, shapes, levels of poverty, and understanding of schooling and academic standards, to pour either their forefathers' and/or God's blessings on the boy and his family.

From somewhere, a once tall and handsome but now leathery and crippled old man edged his way to the front of the crowd. Stopping short of the table near where Phae was seated, he declared, loud and clear, "My son! My son! Come to me! Come to your father." Phae heard the loud but hoarse voice and quickly answered:, "Ntate (father) Peete, good God! You are here?"

"I came, my son, because the voices of your ancestors ordered me to. I have orders to bless you with the horn that has been in your mother's family from the days of Moshoeshoe and the Boer wars."

With that, the old man, Peete, towering in spite of his age, reached into the depths of his leather bag and took out a black, short, shiny, sealed horn. With his now fiery eyes fixed on Phae, he prepared to issue ceremonial instructions.

Signaling Phae to come forward, Peete issued orders to everybody. "Kneel!" he instructed. "Kneel down and never rise until I order you to."

Phae moved forward toward Ntate Peete in expectation—he had never heard or seen a similar ceremony—but knowing from the depths of his soul and without any prior rehearsals or forewarnings the imperatives of Sotho tribal customs.

"My son! My son!" the old man implored, "Come to me." Phae complied. With Phae close to him, the old man dipped his finger into the horn to obtain a substance that he subsequently smeared on Phae's face. The mysterious lotion felt cold as the old man continued speaking. "My son, it is my duty and pleasure to convey to you a message from your ancestors. Please listen carefully, as I will never repeat it."

Concern was evident on Phae's forehead as the old man continued, "I order you to depart the lands of your ancestors as soon as you can and to return only after you have acquired the intellectual tools and powers to help tear us out of apartheid's bondage. To help us out of apartheid's curse you shall never ask: how did my ancestors confront the Boers? Confrontations that are based on following ancestor precedents that never worked are irrelevant. You shall, however, ask: what are the best methods available given current technologies and world power configurations? Abroad, my son, you shall fear nothing."

"There is no evil force in the world worse than what you have confronted here," he continued. "No manmade nor extraterrestrial force of any kind whatsoever should ever scare you. I am authorized to tell you that you shall fear neither lightning nor thunder nor the conspiracies of jealous men." With some faintness in voice he concluded, "Go, my son, to conquer.

"Go open up new paths and doorways for others to follow," he instructed, as he reached, again, into the depths of his leather case for a root. He bit off a piece, chewed it, and spat it back on Phae's face and chest whilst declaring, "Let the curse of our ancestors be upon those who are forcing you to leave. Surely, I am telling you, their cursed evil reign is nearing its end."

Turning to the other visitors, he declared loudly and firmly, "It is finished. Arise!"

Hours after Ntate Peete's dramatic ceremonial address, the last of the guests bid Phae and Nancy goodnight and disappeared into Bophelong's streets. With their disappearance, family privacy was restored, giving Phae the belated needed time to introduce Nancy to his family, first to his mother.

"'Mme (Mme literally means mother or mom), this is Nancy Tau," Phae began. "She has been the subject of most of my letters in the last several weeks," he continued as he stretched his right arm to encircle Nancy's waistline. "Nancy," Phae continued, "is fluent in Sesotho, even though her background, I think, is Tswana. I am sure you two are going to spend hours talking to each other after Nancy has rested overnight."

Phae's mom was transparently glad to meet Nancy. She looked Nancy directly in her eyes and said, "Dearest Nancy, I am truly delighted to meet you! You are such a beautiful-looking young lady! Phae's black-and-white photos didn't catch half the beauty I am seeing now. Can I please hug you?"

Nancy leapt at the opportunity. Within seconds, the two were hugging each other like they were old, established friends. Nothing could have pleased Phae more. Once his mother has welcomed Nancy, his dad's approval was a given. But that had to wait for tomorrow when the two could go to the Bantu Café to meet his father. Tonight his father was not due to reach home until nearly midnight—thirty minutes or so after the family store closed. By then, naturally, Phae, Nancy, and the other members of the family who were not working the store's evening hours would be, hopefully, sound asleep.

Phae's secret prayer for that night—one he wouldn't easily share with Nancy—was that local law enforcement agents would not wake the family up in the middle of the night to check the family's compliance with local rules, especially those stipulating conditions under which Bophelong residents could host guests. When the agents—called municipal police, not to be confused with the SAP, the all-powerful South African police, which were basically the equivalent to the American FBI—did their checks, they would literally kick the doors open and search all parts of the house with flashlight beams, checking for unauthorized guests. They would be as loud and as disruptive as they could be, even in a residence occupied by a distinguished member of the community! What was the rationale behind this?

No one in Bophelong knew for sure, but some surmised that it was simply a tool to keep all blacks aware of what apartheid deemed their uncertain status in urban South Africa.

Urban South Africa, in Afrikaner thinking, belongs to white people. All blacks in urban areas are there at the pleasure of the local municipal administrations. Blacks, the thinking posited, belong to traditional tribal territories; and it was the Afrikaner's God-decreed mission to constantly remind them of that. Phae's prayers were for that reminder to be postponed—just for this one night. And God, in his infinite mercy, granted Phae's prayer.

The Tsolo family and their beloved guest had a quiet, peaceful night. When Phae woke up at 5:30 AM to join his father on his trip to open the store, he set aside a few seconds to thank God for granting him his prayer!

The early-morning trip to the store was revelatory. Since Phae's father did not own a car, he walked to and from the store every day! Phae was never comfortable with this arrangement, but he did not have the means to do anything about it. To his father, walking to and from the store—a distance of two to three miles through one of the world's most dangerous streets without any weapon of any kind to defend himself or his companions—came as naturally as Adam's walks through the corridors of the garden of Eden; both knew deep down that at any given moment God guaranteed their safety! In Jerry's case, God's guarantee held true year after year, crisis after crisis. Incredible as it may sound, Jerry never made a vulgar boast about this fact, not even

during any of his impassioned sermons in that Dutch Reformed Church on Bophelong's main street. Jerry's first words upon seeing Phae so early on a Sunday morning were revealing. "Good God, Phae-Phae! What gets you up so early on a Sunday morning?" he asked.

"Dad, it's so nice to see you!" Phae responded as he rushed to hug his father. "There is no way," Phae continued, "that I am going to be caught sleeping in the morning while you are at work. Never! Today and all the days that Nancy and I are here, I am going

Jeremiah Tsolo, Phae's father. 1960s photo

to give you as much help as I can. Whenever you do not see me next to you in the store, you will know that I am putting the finishing touches on my plans to leave for Lesotho's Pius XII University College."

"That's extremely nice of you, my dear son. As you know, your mother and I can use all the help you can give us. You seem to have grown up. Have you gained an inch or so in height? You also seem to be fit and muscular. Does that mean you are still boxing?" Jerry asked, showing a level of concern and attention to detail that Phae had never seen before.

"Dad," Phae responded, "you are really observant. I have, in fact, gained some weight. When I left for Kilnerton I was a flyweight, hitting the scales at one hundred and twelve pounds. Now I am in the one hundred and eighteen pounds bantam weight division. That's a big change. I am glad you noticed it."

"You are now in the bantam weight division? Why is that worrying me?" Jerry replied. He paused, scratched his forehead, and suddenly exclaimed, "God almighty! That's Sharpeville's Sexton Mabena's division! I am now really glad he is turning pro. I hope you two would never meet in a pro ring."

Phae was really surprised by his father's ability to make such quick logical connections about a sport in which he had only marginal interest. Mabena, Sharpeville's brightest boxing star, was the Vaal's best hope for capturing the professional bantam weight division national championship. He was envied by all boxing enthusiasts who truly believed that if Mabena could get the appropriate training and management, his prospects for winning national and world awards were indisputable. Before Phae could respond, Jerry changed the focus of their discussion sharply.

"Phae," Jerry said unexpectedly, "let's forget about Mabena. Tell me about Nancy. I know given the time that we have you cannot tell me much, but let's make a start nevertheless."

Phae was genuinely surprised. This level of discussion was too new and too strange for him. He was not comfortable with its openness and directness. Had his father changed? How should he handle his new father? Traditionally, discussions relating to love affairs and impending engagements and marriages were first held with an uncle, a "malome" in Sesotho, who would then alert the parents of the developments. An inner voice advised Phae: "This is your dad; level with him." Phae decided to obey the inner voice.

"Dad, in my short life I have fallen in love with only two girls," Phae said. "One is Elizabeth Khosana from Sharpeville, and I am sure that not only have you heard about her and our relationship, but that you have actually met her. Elizabeth, nicknamed 'Ngee,' gave me the love and devotion that fundamentally changed my attitude toward females. The other is obviously Nancy. I am deeply, profoundly torn between the two. I hope you and mom would help tilt my decision one way or the other."

Before Jerry could answer, the Bantu Café loudly announced its presence. They had arrived at the store and half a dozen or so workers en route to Iscor—a major steel manufacturer—were waiting to buy the items they needed before boarding buses to their jobs. With incredible suddenness, a promising father-son dialogue was brought to a screeching halt; customers were now a priority! The discourse was never resumed. Jerry's tight schedule wiped it off the slate.

Beyond helping the family with routines at the store, Phae spent his time showing Nancy places of interest and putting the final touches on his Pius XII University College plans. Needless to say, places of interest in the Bophelong area accessible to people of color were severely limited, enabling Phae to devote more attention to college-related pursuits. He was surprised by the ease and smoothness with which everything proceeded.

The formalities of departure from South Africa to Lesotho in the late 1950s were easy—maybe not to everyone, but definitely to Phae. Without any fuss whatsoever, he obtained pass papers—different from a passport—from the local magistrate's court, entitling him to enter Lesotho, which was then still called Basotholand. As far as Phae could remember, there was no payment, no photos, and no waiting. It was all over within an hour or so.

Having secured the travel papers, Phae's next target became securing financial backing or a scholarship. The only possible source for this was the Isaacson Foundation Fund in Johannesburg. He visited the Fund's office to outline his case. The receptionist at the Fund listened attentively and seemed to be impressed. She told Phae that he seemed to have met all of the Fund's requirements except one—a satisfactory performance in the matriculation examinations. Since Phae never thought of the examinations as obstacles, he strutted out of the Fund's offices a picture of triumphant delight.

The announcement of the Joint Matriculation Board examination results was a nonevent for Phae. In fact, Phae even forgot to buy the local daily newspaper featuring the results. Years later, he was to recall that only one of his friends gave him a congratulatory hug as a result of a newspaper report!

Lesotho is mountainous

To Phae's friends, the results of the examinations were immaterial—almost irrelevant. What was most material and most relevant was the fact of Phae's forthcoming departure for Lesotho. To the gang, his departure conjured up all sorts of wild and romantic pictures. To them, Lesotho was the land of the once-fierce fighters who challenged the Boers to battle and managed, with minimal casualties, to inflict several memorable defeats over their conceited Afrikaner enemies. Yes, Lesotho, the birthplace of Southern Africa's incomparable diplomat, king, and nation-builder Moshoeshoe. It was the land of a people gifted in poetry, music, dance, and horsemanship. This was the land of a people who, battered by a harsh history and geography, managed to retain a national positiveness and pleasantness of manner rarely equaled and probably never surpassed. This was the magnetism of Lesotho; this was its final allure and this is what fascinated the gang. Nyakane's presence and his fluency in the language of the Basothos, Sesotho, added a living vital link to the picture.

Having roamed the often-icy frozen heights of the Lesotho mountains barefooted, with no protective garment other than a tattered blanket and a loin cloth, Nyakane's picture of Lesotho was surrealistic.

"Lesotho is mountainous," Nyakane would declare. "As you drive from Maseru to the interior of the country, it opens up, layer by layer. The mountains unfold right in front of you. You feel you should embrace them, hug them, love them, and yet you know you can't; it's impossible. But your soul would reach out to them in one act of love. You will love the mountains, from the huge, flat, sedimentary rock formations with huge dongas (canyons or ravines) on their foothills …"

As Nyakane's recollections and reconstructions flowed out, the words would drop from his mouth with the rapidity of machine-gun fire. Sometimes one had the feeling that his teeth, tongue, and lips would, in the process, all become entangled in one fantastic, unintelligible knot. When that happened somebody would, as Richard did on this occasion, cry out, "Halt it just there, Nyakane. Tell us about something more ordinary, like your cattle herders."

"Cattle herders? What about the herders?" Nyakane asked impatiently. He hated being interrupted when he was warming up to his favorite topic.

"Yes, herd boys, man. Didn't you tell me the other day that they have trained their cattle stock to obey them, to …" Richard tried to explain, but before he could finish Nyakane announced that he had caught the clue.

"Oh yes, I get you, Ntate (dad/sir in Sesotho)," Nyakane responded. "Before I get too far, I want to make a clarification. Basotho herd boys are not cowboys. Our herd boys in Lesotho are nothing like what you guys have here in Kopanong (South Africa in Sesotho) or what you see in your bioscopes (movies). Our herd boys are nothing like a Durango Kid or Roy Rogers or the Lone Ranger or any of the other cowboys who chase cattle amidst deafening gunfire. No, sir. Further, they are not like your local herd boys here, who are too prone to stone the poor animals into compliance."

"Okay, Nyakane. Get to the point, man," someone cut in impatiently.

"You just stop it," Nyakane warned. "When you are telling your dirty stories about your girlfriends, I never interfere. You just keep quiet," Nyakane ordered. His audience, as if in compliance, was silent, enabling him to continue. "As I was saying, our Lesotho boys have trained their cattle to follow them. How do they do it? Simple. Unbeknownst to you guys, cattle are sensitive to sound pitches. Our herd boys have sensitized their cattle to basically two different whistled pitches. One pitch tells the cattle that its time to go home. When the herders use this pitch, they reinforce it by starting to walk homewards and the cattle soon follow," Nyakane concluded.

"Fantastic!" somebody exclaimed.

"Incredible!" Richard added. "I find this totally incredible. What do you think Phae?"

"Think?" Phae responded. "Boy, me and cattle never reached that level of communication! I was never taught much about what they could or couldn't do beyond towing the plow or providing milk. But for sure I never heard of this type of cattle performance before. It sure beats me. If we could have controlled our cattle during our cattle-herding years the same way, we would have had a fantastic time herding cattle for hours and hours after school and for days during school holidays," he concluded, suggesting that it was time to end discussion of this topic. The others nodded silent approvals. The only area of involvement for the gang in Phae's Lesotho plans was in organizing his farewell party—Bophelong's first!

There was an admirable, methodological thoroughness to the gang's preparation for Phae's farewell party. To Nyakane, the farewell party was to be a party to the "superlative degree." To Richard, it was to be a party such as Bophelong had never seen—a party without precedent, or one that could never be easily equaled or surpassed. It was beyond doubt to be an all-night party, with everyone guaranteed to have a good time. How was this going to be assured?

Simple. A live band contracted from out of town was to provide the main entertainment. Local groups would, intermittently, add a local texture to the entertainment. Food and beverages were to be provided in abundance, while alcoholic beverages were to be severely limited.

The day and the band were chosen. The venue was to be Bophelong's community hall. Phae and his cherished friend, Samuel Mokete Mosiea, plastered posters advertising the party in bold, colorful letters wherever they would be most visible. The local media were issued invitations and requests for publicity. Their response was warm and positive. Food and beverages were collected from homes, stores, and the farmers' market with scant regard to their cost.

By party time on the evening of the appointed day, police had to be called in to control the traffic. That the police cooperated was a testimony to the high regard the local community placed on the event.

The guests arrived punctually—an atypical development. They were all dressed formally, fashionably, and colorfully. Phae couldn't resist taking color photos of the guests, not only as they arrived but in diverse partying settings—dancing, singing, eating, and just having fun. When the band struck the popular dance hit tune, phata-phata, enthusiasm began breaking propriety's bounds left and right. People danced, ate, and, surprisingly, drank until by the early hours of the morning when the cocks started announcing their awakening. By then the party had shed its formality, and the community hall had become littered with human debris in all states of overnight decadence.

In one corner, Nyakane' torso sprawled across a woman's lap in one huge, snoring bundle. Near the beverage stand, two pairs of legs protruded, supported intermittently by empty beer cans. Toward the center of the hall lie a male figure with his mouth and nose half-stuck in a pan of food. On the stage was what appeared to have been members of the performing groups in all stages of sleepy, snoring, careless abandon.

"Yes, it was a party, a hell of a party," Phae recalled as he wrapped his blanket tightly around his 118-pound frame aboard the second-class train sleeper on its way to Bloemfontein and Maseru, the capital city of Lesotho. Pius XII University College was about nineteen miles beyond Maseru. Recalling some lurid details of the farewell party, he smiled quietly to himself in the full knowledge that the messy, unforgettable party was probably the most appropriate ending to a decade in which hell had stalked his destiny with uncanny persistence, leaving a trail of undeserved disfigurements, countless apartheid-era hate-generated deaths, and revenge-seeking plots in its wake.

Chapter 7

Phae had a rare ability to find peace and comfort in unusual places. In his early teens as a cattle herder, he had been able to extract peace and comfort from herding cattle all alone for hours on end, miles from home. In those flat open pastures, the sounds of silence were not academic fictional creations. They were real and even palpable. No wonder then that on this train trip to a strange and unknown land, he found peace and comfort in a second-class, non-white steam locomotive—what his nephew descriptively calls the "choo-choo" train.

That the train was segregated was a nonissue to Phae. His only concern was minor: he couldn't open the windows as widely as he would have liked because widely opened windows let in too much soot! When the train whistled upon approaching a station, the noise was a trifle too intrusive. Otherwise, the second-class compartment was comfortable and conducive to meditation and reminiscing, not only about the immediate farewell party excesses but also about his past and the factors that had influenced it.

Phae's roots were fundamentally rural. Up until 1950, his family and all his ancestors had lived in rural settings. They were cattle and corn farmers, pure and simple. Throughout his elementary school years, Phae had herded cattle after school and on weekends. His family's cycle of schooling and herding cattle only ended in 1950 when his father moved into the new "location" of Bophelong. Why was it called a location instead of a township? The answer is apartheid-rooted: white folks live in townships. Blacks are located where they are easily available to work for whites. Places where they are located are then called locations. Locations are peculiarly South African apartheid-era creations, but the terminology is likely to outlive the ideology.

An unsuccessful effort was made to segregate the blacks according to tribal affiliations within the locations. The effort was born dead. In too many instances tribal identities had been compromised by the interwoven forces of urbanization, industrialization, and education among other things.

A different and more "successful" effort was made to segregate blacks within Bophelong along residential status. There were, on one side, regular home-leasing families. During the early years of Bophelong, black real estate and property ownership was nonexistent. All blacks lived in houses owned by the white municipality of Vanderbijl Park. As long as the black residents paid their rent and utility bills, everything was okay.

A large section of Bophelong was a hostel for black, male contract workers employed by the big firms, such as the world-famous steel-producing giant Iscor. The hostel was occupied exclusively by males from some of South Africa's most remote tribal areas. The existence of an all-male, contract-employees' hostel next to a residential area was a formula for problems and violence that was to bequeath a sad legacy to intra-black urban relations for years to come.

Phae loved Bophelong. The name originates from the Sesotho word for life, "bophelo." Bophelong, then, means a place where there is an active, vibrant life.

In spite of its many weaknesses, the location gave Phae and his family a warm welcome when they moved into the area in December of 1950. Jerry, Phae's father, had made sure that the family's introduction to an urban setting was smooth, even exciting; he surprised them by opening Bophelong's first grocery retail outlet on the eve of their arrival. The outlet, to everybody's but Jerry's surprise, was modern and well-stocked.

On opening day, Christmas of 1950, the Bophelong Bantu Café was glittering with contemporary Christmas decorations and alive with music, and it was jam-packed with an excited clientele eager to buy from a modern, black proprietor with impeccable credentials. That it was a South-African Christmas morning meant that most of the clientele also expected to be given Christmas freebies—and Jerry was more than prepared to accommodate them with colorful balloons, glitter-wrapped candy, and, naturally, home-baked Christmas cakes!

The store and its dramatic opening immediately gave the family a higher status in the community and gave Jerry a platform upon which he built a successful community leadership ladder. Jerry's name and signature was soon on everything of significance in the community. He was the lead preacher in the local Dutch Reformed church. He was the chairman of the township board. He was a leading member of the Bophelong elementary school board. He was also on call whenever private families had difficulties settling their domestic disputes. He was literally everywhere, from five thirty in the morning to eleven at night, Monday to Monday. Was it any wonder that his children nicknamed him "The Mayor?" Whenever any member of the family wanted to see him, they had to meet him at the store or ask for a few minutes with him between his many commitments.

Quite clearly, Jerry's commitments to the community were praiseworthy and admirable, but they were commitments that he honored, unfortunately, at the expense of the family. This was the one sore weakness in the Jerry bubble that was to rear its ugly head at unpredictable times.

Phae was not saddened by his review of his beloved father's lifestyle. Phae felt sorry for his dad. He felt that his dad was caught in a web he couldn't get out of. His father's entrepreneurship was a gem in one context, and a dysfunctional curse in another. Worse, the entrepreneurship lacked a crucial element: modern business management. Whenever a customer requested an item on credit, Jerry would hand the customer the item and accept the customer's verbal promise that he would pay within so many days with no written agreement. No records were kept of the transaction. Jerry figured that knowing and trusting the customer was more important than written contracts. Worse, written contractual commitments were not quite African. To some theorists, Jerry's stand was considered traditional African socialism. To Phae it was tragic. The profit margin in retail is too small to accommodate random acts of African kindness in the form of debts that could not, in all likelihood, be collected. Fortunately for Jerry, the volume of business had for a long while hidden the negative effects of poor management, but for how long could that be sustained?

Another aspect of Jerry's poor management bothered Phae. His father's business was based upon using family members as staff without formal arrangements being made for their reimbursement for the services they rendered. In return for their assistance, members of the family who, at any given time held staff positions at the retail store, were allowed to help themselves to the edibles in the store, again without anyone keeping a record of what was consumed! Needless to say, no records were kept of the hours they had worked or the holidays they had accumulated, and no health or other employee benefits were spelled out anywhere. Phae believed that the Bantu Café was a good example of an emerging Third-World transitional entrepreneurship caught between the old ways and the new.

When Jerry was a successful farmer, his lackadaisical management was hidden by several factors. For example, the payments for the use of land were based on crop yields. Since the white farm owners owned the corn-thrashing machines, they collected their portions immediately after thrashing the corn. There was no need for books or records to be kept. Similarly, the farm assistants Jerry used were paid not in cash but in bags of corn that they had harvested. The farm assistants had no formal vacation or sick days provided for in their unwritten contracts. If any one felt sick they simply informed Jerry, and it was up to Jerry to find a substitute. What about health and retirement benefits? The concepts didn't even exist among Jerry's farming assistants. Incredible as it might seem, Jerry and his farming crew were always happy, kind, keen, and above all else, loyal. They all participated in Tsolo family parties and events as if they were genuine, intimate family members.

Life on the farm had a simplicity and beauty that frequently puzzled Phae. In the comfort of the coal-powered train coach, he tried to figure out the defining features of this simplicity and beauty in daily life. Obviously, his days on the farm were spent out in the veld herding cattle. On the face of it, it was a dull occupation, but on closer examination, there were several moments of challenge, excitement, and enrichment.

When out on the pastures the challenges were many, with most involving how to survive in an environment where snakes and other wild and dangerous animals posed daily hazards. Herd boys had no access to first-aid equipment or medications in the case of bites, cuts, or even the consumption of poisonous roots.

The skies above were sometimes a source of calamities. Phae always recalled a day when a heavy hailstorm battered the area with golf-ball-sized hailstones while his younger brother, Molupe, was alone with the cattle in the fields. The damage to young cornstalks was alarming. Molupe, without cover, was savagely battered. Patches of swelling where the hail had found its mark were all over his body and face. By the time Molupe reached home for safety he was barely recognizable.

A challenge out in the pastures that Phae and his age-mates met with creatively was the challenge of providing snacks for themselves. Most of the time the only way to have a decent snack was to trap one. Birds were difficult to catch. The boys had tried stoning them, but the success rate was too low to be useful. The best method was to trap them. The traps that the boys used were ingenious. Pulling a cord activated the simpler of the traps. The trap itself was usually a bicycle wheel rim covered in wire mesh. One end of the wheel would be on the ground and the other would be about two feet above the ground, supported by a thin pole tied to a long rope. Bird feed—usually crushed corn kernels—would be spread on the ground under the wheel. When enough birds were seen feeding on the kernels below the wheel, the trapper would pull the rope tied to the wheel support. With the support gone, the wheel would collapse on top of the birds below it—without killing them. It was left to the trapper to decide which of the birds he wanted for his snack, and which, if any, were to be set free. If the birds happened to be doves, especially pigeons, they were kept and almost literally adopted into the family. At one stage, Phae's pigeon collection exceeded one hundred birds. Phae loved pigeons. They were beautiful in the diversity of their plumage and dramatic in romance. For Phae, a born collector, pigeons had an attraction that other domestic stock could never match; in addition to their natural biological multiplication, the flock would increase in number by capturing others. One day, four of Phae's pigeons decided to fly westwards. "Were they attracted by the crimson sunset?" Phae wondered. Within thirty minutes they returned, with their numbers having doubled to eight!

Converting live birds to snacks out on the isolated pastures was a challenge for which Phae was adequately prepared. His older brother, Ben, had taught him how to ignite firewood in an improvised barbeque stand when alone on a sunny day in the veld: use a lens to concentrate sun energy enough to ignite the kindling! This required time and concentration—qualities the pastures and Phae had aplenty. When he was in a hurry, Phae always had a box of matches with him. Kindling and firewood were plentiful. The only other thing Phae needed was a piece of wire to suspend the de-feathered bird over the fire. This type of snack usually took about thirty minutes to prepare. Was it tasty? Not always. Some birds seemed to taste saltier than others. Sometimes he would forget to remove the bile before barbequing the bird, which would render it basically inedible.

Snacks made in this fashion had one inherent disadvantage: there were no drinks to down the meats. There was one other more serious disadvantage: if done during the dry winter months, the risk of starting wildfires in the veld was real.

During summer months, crops provided a source for snacks: corn on the cob was plentiful, and watermelons and a type of sweet cane cultivated by local farmers were easily available. Rabbits, porcupines, and other animals that the herd boys often caught were not eaten as snacks—they were taken home for mom to cook! Porcupine catches were extremely rare—herd boys feared them because they were made to believe that porcupines, when attacked, could shoot their quills like arrows!

Toys on the farm were self-made. Most homemade toys were made of wire. Using ordinary wire, Phae and his friends would make cars, trucks, and buses. None of the toys were self-propelling. They all had a device that enabled the owner to push and steer them comfortably while walking or even running. That the boys were inclined to make wire cars sometimes puzzled Phae. Most of the boys were lucky if they had seen more than one car in their life, and few had ever been inside one! Occasionally the boys would attempt to make clay items, but their success rates were invariably low and almost always unsatisfactory.

Going to school was not at all fun to the farming boys. For starters, the schools were all far from their homes. Phae's first school—which he attended at age seven—was more than ten miles away from his home. He had to walk, barefooted, a total of at least twenty miles per day, five times a week!

Throughout his elementary schooling, Phae knew only one boy who owned a bicycle. His name was Boise Makoe. His father owned Bophelong's only commercially usable truck; it was used to sell coal! The Makoes had lived previously in Sharpeville—an older and more urbanized community.

At the end of each school day, Phae had to take his turn herding cattle as soon as he got home. If he had any homework to do, he had to do it at night by the light of a candle or kerosene lamp. Weekends on the farm were spent herding cattle all day long.

With their daily lives rigidly structured, the chances of cattle herders following wrong behavioral inclinations were few and far between. In fact, the first time Phae was ever guilty of any major behavioral wrongdoing—huffing—did not happen until he had moved off the farm to Bophelong. That single incident left an unforgettable mark in Phae's memory.

It was late evening, just before sunset, when Phae met some boys he knew who were huffing benzene. For reasons that Phae couldn't fathom, he decided to experiment. For some time, everything went well. Soon, however, he started hearing melodies coming from the far west. With the melodies came a dramatic change in the appearance of the road surface. The asphalt was transformed into a rubbery, textured carpet. With more huffing a strange phenomena soon appeared: Phae started dying. Slowly. Death started from the bottom of his bare feet. It climbed slowly toward his knees. As Phae saw his body dying on earth, the dead portions were re-emerging on a beautiful white path that curved in front of him like a Nike symbol toward the beautiful blues of what must have been, he thought, heaven.

As his body was slowly dying, Phae saw the beautiful Nike-symbol path stretching away from his feet through the blue skies toward the gates of heaven. Phae was transfigured. He was now half extraterrestrial!

As the dying portion spread to his shoulders and toward his neck, Phae thought his total death was eminent. He was suddenly scared stiff. Once scared, a former herd boy does one thing for sure: run for dear life.

Phae ran fiercely toward the one sure place of absolute safety he knew: home. He ran and ran until finally, and mercifully, he reached home. Upon his arrival, he threw the kitchen door wide open. His mother, Ntlapu, was seated quietly, knitting in the kitchen. Frightened, Phae leaped upon his mom's lap, crying and doubling over in spasms. Ntlapu seemed to have intuitively known what was happening. She comforted her son and offered him a warm glass of home-brewed ginger beer. Incredibly, she never asked Phae what had happened. She was simply glad that her beloved son had found comfort on her lap in his hour of need.

What were the consequences for Phae? Without anyone ever telling him to, he never ever indulged in huffing again!

Phae's peaceful musings and recollections were jarred by the train's arrival at the capital city of Bloemfontein in the middle of the Orange Free State. This was the first major stop it had made since embarking in Vereeniging, so there were quite a few people getting either off or on the train at Bloemfontein. Phae, knowing that the stop was going to take upwards of thirty minutes, took a few steps outside the train to survey the site.

Viewed from the railway station, Bloemfontein was not too impressive. By the time the conductor whistled to alert the passengers of the train's departure, Phae was more than ready to go.

The trip from Bloemfontein to Maseru was uneventful. The landscape was largely flat, dry, and deforested. There were sprawling cattle farms with homesteads boasting windmills and wind chargers long before global warming and the energy crisis made their use fashionable. There was only one visible mountainous outcropping. Phae remembered somebody calling the structure Thaba Nchu (black mountain). Unseduced by the tepid flatness of the Free State, Phae easily resorted to musings about his elementary school days.

When Phae first went to school, his parents were living on a farm in the Vereeniging area that was adjacent to a small section of a town that was then known as Brick and Tile. The Vaal River bordered the farm on the south. On the northern side, the farm was demarcated by a major highway linking Vereeniging to Parys. Phae's first school was several miles away along the highway toward Parys, within a stone's throw of where the highway intersects with the Johannesburg to Sasolburg golden highway. That school predated Bophelong and was closed only when the Bophelong community elementary school opened in the '50s. It was at this small rural school that an incident propelled Phae to make a life-altering promise to himself.

One day Phae saw the school principal, Mr. Nhlapo, whipping a boy who had failed to complete his homework. The frightened boy unashamedly bawled for help. When Phae saw the whipping, he couldn't believe it. He ran to his classroom teacher to report the incident. The classroom teacher, a child-loving mother, hugged Phae tenderly while whispering, "The boy is being whipped because he failed to do his assigned homework." When Phae heard that he made a solemn promise to himself:

"I shall never be caught with my homework incomplete. Never!"

Over time, that promise evolved into a motto: I shall never place myself in a position where a teacher or an authority figure could have cause to whip me for poor performance in any of my academic subjects or in my job. This promise, made in his early teens, became the governing credo of his life.

In spite of his promise, Phae was whipped once before completing grade six. The setting was a choir rehearsal at the Bophelong Elementary School. The teacher caught a boy's voice that was out of tune. Not knowing who the boy was or why the boy was out of tune, he decided that all of the boys in the choir were to be whipped for the discordant note. When it came to Phae's turn, he blocked the "whip"—this time it was really a quarter-inch-thick carpenter's ruler—with his left hand, just as he was taught to do in the gym. The ruler hit a bone, and in minutes the swelling was visible on Phae's left hand. That swelling, Phae decided, was the hard evidence his father would need to follow up investigating this abominable brutality of the teacher.

The belief that his father—chairman of the school board—would act retributively was naïve. Phae found out that in the transitional culture of Bophelong, adults were entitled to punish any child anywhere for any inappropriate behavior, real or imagined.

A metallic tap on the train door shook Phae out of his reminiscences. The tap was followed by these words from the white ticket inspector: "Tickets, please! We are now approaching Maseru. Please make sure you have all your belongings together."

Phae did not fail to notice that the announcement was, for the first time, in English instead of Afrikaans. "Why?" he wondered. "Is it because we are now approaching the British Commonwealth of Nations Protectorate of Basotholand where English was the official language?" Whatever the answer, Phae admitted to himself that he was now poised for a major change. For starters, the white ticket inspector had said "please." No Afrikaner official had ever shown that level of courtesy to blacks! Phae was immediately intrigued.

Within minutes, the coal-powered locomotive slowed to a walking pace. Phae opened the train window, and, to his utter surprise, ahead of him were the mountains of Basotholand in bold relief! The train stopped briefly before crossing a tepid river that marked the boundary between South Africa and the protectorate to allow for the opening of the gates leading into the new territory. It was soon after that Phae saw the significant welcome to Basotholand message written in large print for all to see:

"Basotholand: Kena Ka Khotso / Enter In Peace."

This was not the first time that Phae had entered a foreign country. He had visited Mozambique during his Kilnerton stay. Mozambique had a no border-entry sign as evocative as Basotholand's. Could any other country have had a more endearing welcoming message? The formalities surrounding entry into Basotholand were minimum— almost token formalities in January 1960. Within minutes, Phae and all the other passengers were inside Maseru, the capital city of Basotholand, which would soon revert to its historic name: Lesotho.

In no time, Phae and the other arriving passengers were rushed at by Maseru's transportation entrepreneurs who were offering taxi services to the bus stations. It was a little confusing and hectic, and

Phae had to tell himself a few times: "Calm down, kid. Everything is going to be fine!"

He finally settled for an entrepreneur whose minibus and crew seemed acceptable. In seconds, Phae's luggage was tossed on top of the minibus. The minibus took off, noisily but clearly, driven by hands that were familiar with the local terrain. The drive through Maseru to the main bus terminus was brief but revealing of local conditions.

Maseru was unlike any capital city or town that Phae had ever seen. For starters, it had only about two miles of tarred roads! There were no traffic lights anywhere along the main street. There were also no buildings that Phae could recall that were higher than two stories. None of the big retail or hotel chains were anywhere to be seen. In fact, the only hotel was Maseru Inn, an unforgettable place to Phae because its thatched roofing was extremely well done; he even thought it glistened! "Isn't that a crazy thought?" Phae whispered to himself. "How could thatching glisten?" The only other structure that caught Phae's attention was a cathedral—most likely Catholic. This was located at the extreme eastern end of the capital city proper, just beyond the only wide traffic circle intersection of the roads linking Maseru to the rest of the country. The cathedral was built of solid limestone blocks that gave the building a solidity and a guaranteed longevity that tempted Phae to make the following initial entry in his Lesotho notebook: "Maseru, Roman Catholic (?) cathedral—more than worth visiting."

The main bus stop in Maseru was an open lot of between five and ten acres. It had no passenger conveniences of any kind whatsoever. No bathrooms. No sitting benches. No sun or rain covers. Nothing. It was just a big, dusty lot with buses of all descriptions, colors, and luggage-carrying capabilities. There were no signs indicating where to stand for buses going to any particular destination. Instead, bus assistants went from one potential passenger to another informing them of their route and destination. If their bus was going your way, you either hopped on it immediately or were shown the dusty patch where you could catch it. There was clearly an air of intense capitalistic competition between the various advocates of routes that gave the whole experience a freshness and vitality unmarred by the occasional dusty clouds blown about by intermittent breezes.

Phae soon found the bus of his choice; it was colorful and

overloaded with all sorts of luggage, including live fowls! Its destination was Mafefoane, a village in a valley popularly called Roma, a Sesotho variant of the word "Rome" or "Roman." It was called this in part because the Catholics had huge establishments within it, including the highly esteemed Pius XII University College that was nineteen miles from Maseru. It turned out those miles were some of the most eventful Phae had ever experienced. Within less than thirty minutes of departure, a passenger requested the bus driver to stop so that she could go to the bathroom! Since there was neither a building nearby nor any trees to provide some privacy, Phae was intrigued. The woman got out of the bus, walked a few paces, and then simply squatted in full view of everybody in the bus. However, except for her profile in a squatting position, there was nothing inappropriate to see; the woman was well covered by her wide, loose-fitting skirt and colorful, traditional Basotho blanket!

A few miles later the bus had to stop again. A passenger had an item to deliver at an approaching village! No one protested or expressed any form of disapproval. Everybody continued chatting about their village interests peacefully, oblivious to the dictates of time.

When the bus finally arrived at the Pius XII University College campus, a passenger suggested that the bus driver should drive into the campus and stop by the main administrative building, since Phae had heavy luggage and was unfamiliar with the area! The driver complied without a murmur of protest from any of the by now dust-covered passengers. Phae thanked them profusely in Sesotho in what they thought, as Americans would say, was a funny accent! After disembarking and getting his luggage together, he paid the bus driver for his portion of the trip and gave the driver's assistant a liberal tip. Somehow everybody on the bus seemed to have seen this and known what was happening, and they all loudly applauded Phae!

Phae's initial encounter with Pius XII University College was filled with excitement. Phae loved everything he saw during this first visit. First, he was impressed by the overall setting. Pius XII University College was located inside a deep valley that was walled on three sides by massive limestone mountains. Beyond the limestone mountains, one could see the outlines of other mountains that were most likely of volcanic origin judging by their conic shapes. The total view was stunning. Phae could not recall ever having been similarly impressed by a landscape.

The administrative offices where he had disembarked were part of a multistoried building that, on its extreme right, housed the Oblates monastery, and on its extreme left, the male students' dormitory. The women's dormitory was a multistoried, nicely designed building that was located just under a quarter mile east of the administrative offices. Between the two big structures were the food services, including the main dining hall. A small community of detached, single-story houses provided accommodation for the teaching and senior administrative staff. Another detached structure contained the library, physics laboratory, and science classrooms. A chapel was located on the eastern edge of the campus.

All of the buildings were constructed of massive limestone rock blocks that had been dug from the surrounding mountains, enabling the structures to merge into the landscape. On this January afternoon, the entire place had an aura of peace and tranquility that Phae adored. He soaked it in for several minutes before walking to the administrative offices to introduce himself. He was greeted by a Sesotho-speaking administrative representative who warmly welcomed him to Pius XII University College.

After unremarkable introductory remarks, Phae was led to his dormitory on the second floor. The dormitory was huge, with a capacity to accommodate at least ten people. On the day of his arrival, he was the only one there; the others were expected to begin arriving the following day, with classes due to start the next week on Monday. The knowledge that he was the first to occupy the dorm was an empowering feeling. Now he would be the one who would introduce the newer arrivals to the dorm. As the first arrival, Phae had the privilege and right to choose the exact location for his bed, wardrobe, and study desk.

The spot he chose for his bed was typical Phae; he placed it in the corner, hugging two walls with their huge windows facing a vista of flat-topped, layered limestone mountains to the west and a chain of cone-shaped, manifestly volcanic high mountains to the east. The western view still showed signs of the massive stone excavations that had been undertaken during the construction of the university's impressive structures. Not too far from the quarry was a Basotho village boasting the typical, traditional Basotho architecture of thatched homesteads. The tranquility of the village setting hid its capacity to evoke extreme emotional reactions during open, mountainside political campaigns.

A city Mafef's political rally. Pius XII College is located within the same Roma valley.

Not only did the spot he chose for his portion of the dorm offer him the best views, it also partially protected him from disturbances by those who would inevitably be frequently coming in and out of the dorm; it was the furthest spot from the doors.

Once he had decided on his spot within the dorm, his next assignment loomed with some amount of urgency—choosing his bed and especially his mattress. Mattresses, Phae knew, determined more than anything else how comfortable one would be while sleeping. Any mattress he was going to use had to pass a test for firmness, comfort, and hygiene. Why hygiene? He had had an unfortunate encounter with bed bugs at a guest cottage in Mozambique during Kilnerton's year-end tour of the place in 1958. His search for bed bugs was meticulous; no crease in the mattress was overlooked. That the Pius XII mattress passed his tests was a resounding affirmation of the positives aspects of this well-located oasis of peace and tranquility.

After settling in, Phae decided to take a tour of the campus before the expected crowds would begin to arrive the following day. The first distinctive feature he noticed about the area, besides the landscape, was the mid-January coolness. January is supposed to be a warm to hot month in South Africa, but this valley was cool; it was no wonder then that most of the passengers on the bus had worn blankets! The explanation for this was given by the first priest he met on the campus—the Reverend Father McCarthy, a member of the Oblates Order in Canada. He had volunteered for a few years' service at Pius XII. Father McCarthy was transparently glad to meet Phae.

"Did you say your name was Donald?" the reverend priest asked.

"Yes, Reverend Father!" Phae replied, fully aware that in this new context he was going to prefer being known by his formal name. That was simply part of the new transformation he was undergoing.

"Thanks!" the priest responded, adding, "Do you prefer to be called Don or Donald?"

"In all honesty, Father, I really do not mind," Phae explained. "All my life I have been called by my nickname, Phae. My grandfather calls me Senyaka-nyaka. It was in Kilnerton—the boarding high school I attended in the Transvaal—that people started calling me Don, and now I find myself responding indifferently to either," he concluded.

"Well, well! For sure I cannot call you either Phae or Senya—how did you say it? Senyaka-nyaka? What a mouthful! What does it mean, by the way?" the priest asked.

"To the best of my knowledge," Phae responded, "it means, broadly, the complex one, with implications that the complexity has a high capacity to lead to troublesome situations."

"Are you by any chance Catholic?" the priest asked.

Phae should have prepared for that question months ago, but he hadn't. Now he was caught in a tight corner. After a moment's hesitation he answered, "I am new to Catholicism. I would like to answer you affirmatively and say definitely yes, but I am fully aware that there is a lot I need to know before I could make that claim without qualifiers."

"Luckily, in your new setting," Father McCarthy responded, "you will have ample time and scope to deepen your Catholicism. And, if you don't mind my saying so, I will always be available to be of assistance."

Phae heaved a big sigh of relief. It hadn't taken long for Father McCarthy to put him in a tight corner! He was glad, though, that he had given the priest an honest answer. Phae's immediate concerns were simple. He wanted to find answers to the following questions: Why is it so cool in this part of the world? Could Father McCarthy give him more information about Pius XII University College? What was the size of the student body? Where did they come from? Was this college racially mixed?

Father McCarthy was ready with the answers. "Pius XII is a small university college," he explained. "Its student body is under four hundred. Most of the students are from South Africa and are," he hesitated before saying it, "black." Father McCarthy thought there were a few—he again hesitated before saying it—colored and Indian students, but he was not sure of their number. Phae's spontaneity interrupted the holy priest.

"Father," he asked, "am I detecting caution in your mentioning the racial composition of the student body?"

The priest paused, looked at Phae for a few seconds, and then continued. "Whites were fewer; last year there was only one white male student. He was from South Africa," he said. The two walked quietly for some time before the priest resumed the conversation. "You say you detected a note of caution when I was mentioning the racial and geographic composition of the student body?" he asked. "You don't have to answer. It is an extremely sensitive point among many. For starters, racial classifications are complex issues with our student body. For example, our staff distinguishes between two concepts: people of color and colored people. To most of the staff, people of color are invariably black and African. Colored people, a racial classification unique to South Africa, refers to a distinct racial group—a mixture of whites, meaning the Dutch descendants we now all call Afrikaners, and any other non-European racial combinations you can dream of, as long as you keep in mind one strong likelihood that probably more than ninety-nine percent of these are likely to be of African origin. The coloreds have a common denominator; they all speak Afrikaans and have a distinctly Afrikaner cultural heritage, but they are not, under South African law, Afrikaners! And they definitely are not classified as white. They belong to a new, uniquely South African category: coloreds.

They did not exist before the Dutch landed on the Cape coast in 1652. Now, what about whites; who are they? Most South African whites are clearly Afrikaner. The next big group consists of descendants of British immigrants who arrived in South Africa during the beginning of the nineteenth century, who initially settled in the eastern Cape Province.

"The British," he continued, "after their arrival, kept their traditions, language, and views of government's role in society—even colonial society—an attitude which, as you must know, led to ongoing conflicts between the two, culminating in the 1830s departure from the Cape Province of the Afrikaner in a movement history calls the Great Trek. The Great Trek deepened the divide between the Afrikaner and the English that history has never—and may never—healed. Needless to say, the Great Trek did not lead to newer, warmer relations between the intruders and the native communities of the time who were the original occupants of the lands the Afrikaner trekked into, but you likely know more about that part of the story than I do."

"You are probably right, Father," Phae responded self-consciously. "I majored in history in high school and also during my one year at the Bantu Normal College, east of Pretoria, where I did some BA level correspondence courses with the Pretoria-based University of South Africa. Even though that may be the case, I still would love to hear your version of our story. Before you go too far, Father, can you backpedal to where you showed caution in mentioning the tribal factor while outlining the composition of the college's student body?"

Father McCarthy stopped and looked at Phae with searching, penetrating eyes before he continued. "To understand my caution," he explained, "you may need to be empathetic. When I first came here, I assumed all Africans were one homogenous block. This view became entrenched by the propaganda literature of the Pan Africanist movement. However, since my arrival, I have found reality to be substantially different. Before I proceed, please tell me, do you belong to a South African political party?"

The question caught Phae completely off guard. He hesitated for a split second before declaring, "Yes, Father. I am by conviction a Pan Africanist."

"Thanks for being so straight forward," the priest replied, adding, "Something in your demeanor gave me the impression that you might be. It's easier for me to understand Pan Africanism than any of the Marxism rampant within the African National Congress—the party whose derogators sometimes call 'the Charterists.' However, I am afraid that Pan Africanism leads to naïve assumptions about the ease with which you can get along with anyone who is African, what you Pan Africanists call 'sons and daughters of the soil.' In so many ways, it is like expecting me to get along well with anyone simply because they have a European heritage. Unfortunately it is not so, and never was so, and may never be so.

"Take, for example, the Afrikaner. They trace their immediate origins to Europe—that's the only thing we share in common. I have nothing else in common with an Afrikaner beyond the superficial similarity in skin color. Similarly, you may find you share only skin color in common with the folks from the Rhodesias. And that's the furthest I will go on this topic for now. After a year or so of exposure to life on this campus, I would love to revisit this topic with you," the Reverend Father concluded, signaling politely that it was time for them to part.

"Thank you, Reverend Father," Phae replied. "I truly appreciate your talking to me and look forward to more of the same in the future," he concluded while warmly hugging the priest good-bye.

Earlier Father McCarthy had unwittingly drawn Phae's attention to an aspect of the composition of the Pius XII University College student body that was to play a major role in Phae's life on this campus; a small but significant percentage of the black student body came from north of the Limpopo River, from the areas known as Northern and Southern Rhodesia and Malawi. Father McCarthy thought the students from the Rhodesias played a role disproportionate to their numbers in the daily life of the student body.

"What was the source of their influence?" Phae had asked.

Father McCarthy was not sure, but he said that some students suggested that the underlying cause was simple—relative financial power. The students from the north had what appeared to be more power simply because they were, relatively speaking, far better off financially than others. They were all attending school on scholarships that were politically motivated, especially those from Southern Rhodesia where the government was pushing an ideology called "partnership." The liberal scholarships allowed them much more spending money, which enabled them to live a life of comparative luxury on the campus.

Phae later found a confirmation of this when he heard that Rhodesian male students viewed taking South African black girls out as "feeding the poor masses"—a remark that provided the major impetus to a revolt that Phae led against "the Rhodesians" during his undergraduate years.

Father McCarthy's explanation for the comparative coolness of the local climate, in contrast, had been simple. Basotholand was the highest point in all of southern Africa. In Africa, as in many other parts of the world, altitude determines the climate. Father McCarthy made sure to warn Phae: "If you think it's cool now, you have quite a few surprises coming."

Phae's first supper at Pius XII was uneventful. The dining hall was almost empty. While supper was unremarkable, it was a definite improvement over Kilnerton. Further, the cooking staff was comprised of nuns—some called them "sisters"—giving one the feeling that their commitment to quality foods was higher than average. But more than anything else, staff and students were served the same dinner! Now, if that's not a guarantee of quality, what could be?

After supper Phae walked back to the dorm. He was literally the only student in his section of the dormitory. There was an almost divine silence around the place, a silence Phae never remembered having encountered either at Kilnerton or the Bantu Normal College, east of Pretoria, where he spent 1959 making the final preparations for Pius XII University College. The Bantu Normal College and Pius XII University College shared three things in common: they were small, vulnerable, and affiliated with the University of South Africa—Africa's largest correspondence university.

The course work that Phae completed at the Bantu Normal College was transferable to Pius XII University College, enabling Phae to complete course work at the latter institution in record time. When Phae reached the door to his second-floor dorm after climbing the stairway—elevators were an unknown luxury here—he paused, imagining how all the others in the days to come would be entering the dorm. During that short pause, he discovered more advantages accruing to him by his early arrival and his choice of bed space. On a moonlit night, the view of the mountains against the sky was gorgeous from his bed. It was a view and a setting conducive to what he loved most: quiet study while others snored the night away.

Before getting into bed he finished unpacking and making final arrangements defining his section of the dorm. For his desk and book stand he chose the best in the dorm and soon had his books neatly arranged. His bedside lamp stand was carved out of the twisted trunk of an oak tree that he had always kept next to his bed. This, he knew with boyish impishness, was going to be a source of endless speculation.

It was not until well near midnight when Phae finally closed his eyes to sleep. Little did he know that this was to be in many ways his first night in exile.

"The gorgeous silence of the early mornings in the Roma valley is a gigantic conspiracy to keep unburdened souls sleeping longer," Phae thought as he slowly removed the woolen cap that he used to cover his head and eyes whenever and wherever he slept. With the cap tossed to the side of the bed, Phae took his first early morning look at the dorm and the campus as viewed from his windows. The dorm still impressed him by its size, its wide windows with minimal curtains, and cleanliness. He made sure the experience sunk into his psyche, just in case some unknown and maybe unpredictable event were to prove that the entire experience was a hoax. Before long, though, strange sensations in his tummy told him it was breakfast time. He checked his wristwatch; it was eight o'clock and time for breakfast—the one meal Phae rarely missed. Soon he was on his way to the food services center where all meals were served.

The atmosphere at the food services center was considerably different. Several students must have arrived either overnight or early this morning and were now more than halfway finished with their breakfasts. The menu choices were modest but appetizing, consisting of the usual choices of cold cereals, hot cornmeal porridge cooked to the consistency of a smoothie, and bacon, sausages, juices, coffee, tea, and—to Phae's pleasant surprise—fresh, ripe peaches. It was a self-serve setup unless, of course, you had problems with the menu, in which case the nuns, who inconspicuously staffed the place, were ready to help.

After Phae loaded his tray, he deliberately targeted a table occupied by three men who least resembled anyone Phae had encountered before. They were formally dressed, looked taller and darker, and spoke English with a distinctly unfamiliar accent. They were clearly comfortable with their environs, a clue that suggested to Phae they had been enrolled here a year or longer. When Phae approached their breakfast table, they all paused and looked at him with inquiring eyes, which Phae took as an invitation to initiate a conversation.

"Hi, guys!" Phae began unreservedly. "I'm Phae. That's what folks back home call me! Over here you are at liberty to call me by my formal name, Donald or Don. I'm brand new to this place. I arrived last night and spent my first night in an empty second-floor dorm." He stretched his right hand to greet his first contact, a guy who seemed to be the natural leader of the small group. After a very brief hesitation the guy responded.

"Glad to meet you, Phae," he replied. "I'm Edison Zvobgo. I'm from Southern Rhodesia, the future Zimbabwe, may I add. I have been here for a few years and would be glad to introduce you to my friends here who are as new to the place as you are." Edison proceeded to introduce the others. They were all from the same country. Four, it turned out were Shona, and the other two were Ndebeles. Phae had never heard a Shona word before, but he knew that Ndebele had a lot in common with the South African Zulu language.

A more social member of the group, a guy from Salisbury, the capital city of Southern Rhodesia, stood up and embraced Phae with a warmth that was at once reassuring and a harbinger of things to come. "I am," the guy declared with touching spontaneity, "Chris, Christopher Mushongwa. Welcome to Pius XII University College. Believe me, you are going to love it here."

"Thanks, Chris," Phae responded, adding, "See you guys later. I'm going to waltz over to the next table."

"See you later," the guys from the Rhodesias declared as they bid Phae good-bye. "Strange," Phae thought on his way to the next table. "These Rhodesian moneyed guys don't seem as uppity as I expected. Let's see if my current impressions stand the test of time," he mused.

The occupants of the next table were almost all equally new to the scene. One was clearly Indian and the others appeared to be coloreds. Phae's interactions with Indians in the past had been limited to transactions in retail stores. Phae's folks back home loved shopping at Indian stores, where "bargains" were plentiful and customers were given material incentives—what Phae's mom called "mbasela"—for the purchases they made. More than just knowing Indians in shopping settings, Phae had also been to an Indian wedding in Durban!

As for coloreds, Phae had met just a few in his life. For starters there were none living in Bophelong—apartheid forbade that. Phae had bumped into a few in Evaton during visits with his grandparents. Evaton was located north of Bophelong and had been made easily accessible to Phae by the newly constructed Golden Highway that connected the two areas. Evaton was an unusual area where blacks and coloreds not only lived together but also owned real estate! Apartheid's efforts to change this never succeeded. Since Phae's visits with his grandparents had been brief, he could never claim to "know" any coloreds on the basis of those visits.

His approach to the Indians/coloreds table was clearly cautious. Why? In South African law, coloreds are assigned a higher social status than blacks and are therefore entitled to considerably more privileges. Phae knew to assume that all coloreds defined their status vis-à-vis blacks in terms of apartheid's stipulations would be preposterous.

Even with that qualifier, an inner voice prompted: be careful. Inner promptings, however, never deterred Phae.

Before Phae could stretch out his right hand for introductions, the Indian guy beat him to it. "Hi!" he joyously declared. "Welcome to our table! I'm Bob, Bob Hira. I'm new to Pius XII. What about you?" he inquired with surprising exuberance.

"I arrived yesterday," Phae replied.

"Know what?" Bob said. "We arrived early this morning. In fact, our travel bags and suitcases are still unopened. Worse, we haven't had a chance to change from what we wore yesterday all day long."

Phae, never one to miss an opportunity for humor, reached out desperately into his back pocket, retrieved a handkerchief, and immediately covered his mouth and nose while announcing, "You didn't have to be so explicit! I still haven't had my breakfast!"

This comment led to an outburst of laughter from Bob Hira's friends. In seconds, the racial representatives of Pius XII, who were all keen to share in the joke, crowded around the table. The mirth making would most likely have gone on indefinitely had not one of the nuns intervened with a reminder that the food services would be closing shop in fifteen minutes. Everybody immediately settled down to the serious business of eating their breakfast.

The after-breakfast scenario was fast and furious, as more and more students arrived. Their means of transportation to the campus were an interesting mixed bag. Two Basotho students simply walked in from a nearby village. Most used a variety of public transportation, including trucks without covers. The latter were a sad sight to see, as the dust from the Lesotho dirt roads changed the colors of their clothes by powdering them with fine, fairly uniform layers of dull, yellow sand. Those who didn't have their heads covered were a sadder looking bunch.

Four of the "seniors"—those in their fourth and hopefully final year at the college—arrived in what was clearly an antique-classic jalopy. Phae was never able to determine the year or exact make of the car, nor whether it was insured or licensed in Lesotho. After its arrival, the jalopy was parked in front of the dorm and remained stationary for weeks, maybe months. Clearly its ownership had little to do with utility and everything to do with its function as a status symbol.

Students assigned to Phae's dorm didn't start arriving until late in the afternoon—and almost all of them came from Swaziland. The first to arrive was a male student whom Phae grew to like and admire with the passage of time; his name was Timothy Zwane. Phae called him Tim, and he called Phae by his formal name. Tim was never a fast operator. Whatever he had to do was planned slowly and meticulously. Even his conversational tone was slow, deliberate, and frequently hesitant. You see, Tim had to think carefully before he acted. Was that traditional Swazi?

Even though he was inclined to thinking ponderously like a traditional conservative, Tim's politics were against the status quo in Swaziland. He thought that the days of monarchical dominance of Swazi political, economic, and social life should be terminated as soon as possible. Tim had to be careful, however, to whom he expressed some of his concerns with the Swazi political system. The Swazi royalty he wanted to reform had close adherents on this small campus. Most of those who had monarchical links shared the same surname; they were all called Dlamini. Well over sixty percent of the students from Swaziland were known to be either Dlaminis or closely related to them. To crown it all, one of the thirty-five girls on campus, it turned out, was a Swazi princess! Another had studied for a year or two at an American university and was prone to start her speeches with "we in the States"—an uppity superficiality that Phae found most abhorrent.

The next day was a Sunday, a day that Phae always associated with the Biblical seventh day; a day to be kept holy, and, more specifically, the day to attend church services. At Pius XII University College, keeping the seventh day holy by attending Catholic worship services was a given. Worship in the college's small chapel was, on this Sunday, fairly routine. What was not routine, however, was Phae bumping into Father McCarthy after worship. After exchanging routine greetings, Father McCarthy touched upon the fundamentals. "Donald, what did you think of the sermon?" he asked.

"Most interesting, Father," Phae replied nonchalantly.

"Can you please be more specific?" Father McCarthy asked with deepening seriousness.

"I was interested in the section dealing with Immaculate Conception," Phae replied, a little nervously. Father McCarthy must have noticed Phae's nervousness. His follow-up question targeted a core weakness in Phae's Catholicism—the fact that it was shallow.

"What do you think Immaculate Conception refers to?" the priest pressed.

Phae was caught. His Catholicism had not touched on some key fundamentals. He truly did not know—as any genuine Catholic is supposed to know—what Immaculate Conception referred to. He admitted the same to Father McCarthy, who mercifully reminded Phae, "Remember what I promised you when we first met? This is the best place to deepen all aspects of your Catholicism. Let me know how I can help you achieve this goal." And with that, the Reverend Father McCarthy bid Phae good-bye.

Phae heaved a big sigh of relief. Later, he casually flung himself down on his bed in the dorm; with his eyes roaming the mountainous landscape he made an important decision. Beginning as soon as possible, he was going to study Catholicism with seriousness and determination. He would never let Father McCarthy or anyone else embarrass him about his Catholicism. The first day the college library was open, Phae went searching for appropriate introductory literature into Catholicism. The librarian, a nun, was both impressed and helpful. Within weeks, the entire Pius XII University College establishment was familiar with Phae's name and religious curiosity.

The first Monday following Phae's arrival was devoted to administrative routines, including registration, dorm assignments, familiarization with classroom procedures—including those in the library and science laboratory—food services routines, and behavioral expectations on campus. The Oblates were clearly and indisputably good at executing all of these with an impressive finesse. By dinnertime, it seemed, everybody was comfortably accommodated and felt quite at home.

At no stage of the Pius XII University College introductory proceedings did Phae or any of the students he interacted with feel fearful of secret initiation rites that students with seniority status may have been tempted to administer. Instead of exhibiting inhibitions because of initiation concerns, the new arrivals were full of enthusiasm and positive expectations.

At supper on Monday, Phae had a chance to see most of the students and staff who were to feature in his first year at the college. He felt most comfortable with them and the spiritual ambience of the place. In spite of this, there were some minor and not insignificant concerns that hovered around Phae's thinking.

One persistent intruder in his thoughts had to do with girls on the campus, who were few and far between. Phae's actual body count of those who had supper fell below forty—the lowest number of girls at any institution that Phae had attended up to this point. Of the few girls there, Phae thought, probably two-thirds had been here before him, and so were his seniors and most likely beyond reach for dating purposes. Far too many males would be attempting to court the remaining third who were conceivably eligible for him to date. How could Phae gain an edge over the competition, especially since most of the new arrivals he met were from established and therefore more sophisticated cities such as Johannesburg, Cape Town, Durban, and Salisbury?

Pius XII University College, ladies' dorms

Phae sought the answer the way he knew best: by returning to basics and telling himself, "Prioritize! Prioritize, kid! You came to Pius XII University College because it offers the best academic opportunities for a black student in this part of the world.

"Pursuit of academic excellence is therefore an unquestionable priority, regardless of the gender composition of the student body."

The next of the personal priorities that Phae examined was his physical fitness and boxing. Up until last year when he won the Northern Transvaal Amateur Bantamweight Championship while enrolled at the eastern Pretoria Bantu Normal College, boxing had been his major vehicle toward physical fitness and—as he found at Kilnerton—recognition and respect. This year, however, he was at the university of his choice, and the quest for academic excellence was not consistent with the pursuit of boxing glory. In fact, Phae thought boxing could be counterproductive; brain damage from punches could lead to strokes and compromise his intellectual performance.

With this awareness, Phae decided with incredible clarity and determination: "Today I am going to retire my boxing gear, and tomorrow I will restring my tennis racket and pursue fitness via tennis, especially since the Roma valley campus has well-kept clay courts." The following day, with his tennis racket restrung to specifications, Phae joined three male students who were practicing at the courts. They were glad to welcome him as a fourth player, enabling them to upgrade their status from "Canadian" to a genuine doubles game.

Dick Stevens "addressing" Basotho children with Roma Valley clearly defined in the background

One of the tennis players impressed Phae with the smoothness and precision of his basic strokes. His serves were also excellent. After practice Phae reached out to him. He responded warmly. His name was Dido Diseko. He was from Bloemfontein in the Orange Free State, a city recognized as one of the four capital cities of South Africa. Phae soon found that not only did he love Dido's style of play, once outside the courts he liked his social deportment, including his suggestion at the end of tennis practice that the four should go for snacks at the students' tuck shop.

To Phae's surprise, when the cashier told Dido the cost of the snack order for four, Dido reached for his wallet to pay. Phae reacted instantaneously; he stretched his right hand beyond Dido's and told the cashier he would pay. His outstretched arm revealed his notorious boxer's knuckles—a sight that caused Dido's eyes to pop out in surprise.

"Wait, Jacque! Are you a boxer?" Dido asked. For reasons no one ever quite understood, Dido called all the guys he liked "Jacque."

Phae was caught off guard. He hesitated for a split second and then bounced back. "Yes, up until yesterday," he explained. "I have been a boxer from early childhood. Boxing was my sole means to physical fitness initially and catapulted me, in Bophelong and Kilnerton, to fame and offers to turn pro. But yesterday, after careful consideration, I decided that the risks inherent in boxing were inconsistent with my academic pursuits, and I packed up my boxing gear. Henceforth, I intend to give tennis a good try, and with guys like you around, I'm bound to do well."

Dido looked at Phae, smiled with surprising coyness, and then said, "Jacque, I truly wish to welcome you to the world of tennis. Not only can one use tennis as an instrument to better one's health, but in my experience I have also found tennis to be a key to winning friends wherever there are courts." After pausing for a few seconds, he added a sentiment that Phae would never forget: "This, Jacque, I must tell you: tennis-based friendships last forever!"

Chapter 8

Before 1960, Bophelong was in fact and in truth a political write-off. If its streets seethed with political discontent, it was a discontent that was disjointed, disorganized, and apparently purposeless. Worse, the discontent frequently exploded in what appeared to be senseless acts of anger against its own—an anger that frequently assumed a brutal and savage form.

It was the sad fate of Bophelong to witness with exasperating frequency scenes of barbaric murders executed with weapons that were as lethal as they were frequently primitive. Of the primitive weaponry, none was handled with more expertise and devastating effects than knives, whether crude and self-made or sleek, sharp, and brand named. True, local sleeks—Tsotsis, as most called them—were not adept in the more exotic knife-handling skills like knife throwing, but they sure knew where to aim on the human body to disfigure, cripple, or worse, kill.

The essence of victory in a knife fight lay in speed. Of all the variables in determining the outcome of a street fight, speed was the most decisive. When the speed of attack was accompanied with exactness of aim, the size or strength of the victim did not matter. On the contrary, it was often true that the bigger the victim, the easier it was for the assailants. It was easier to find the mark on a Goliath, some claimed!

In the heat of a street battle, a fairly typical Bophelong kid would be transformed dramatically into an efficient, murderous machine that moved with the rapidity of a cheetah and the exactness of a cobra. As heirs to Tshaka, king of the Zulus, whose nineteenth-century edict declared that soldiers returning from the battlefield with wounds on their backs should be executed for cowardice, these youngsters would face their victims head-on and stab them—right where it mattered.

Born and bred where the official government creed upheld the cheapness of black lives, some of the local youth embraced violence without any regard for social censure or official retaliation from law enforcement. Not infrequently, a youth would declare before murdering someone: "I am going to kill you. After killing you, I will serve nine months in jail." Everybody knew that was the average penalty for black manslaughter. The murder of a white victim, whatever the extenuating circumstances, was a tale of a different sort. The penalty for that crime ranged from life imprisonment to the hangman's noose. Not much of a range, is it?

While the knife was the characteristic weapon of black urban adolescents, adults, especially new arrivals from the Bantustans and the adjacent territories, tended to depend on a wider array of armaments: the nineteenth-century perfected assegai, the knobkerrie, the big stick—called "koto" in Lesotho—the "needle"—a weapon so lethal that few ever saw it—and not infrequently, the short, stabbing spear of the post—Tshaka Zululand.

Shootings were a rare occurrence and were often reserved for sophisticated situations. A good example of this was a report in the print media that a recent payroll holdup had been staged by six men armed with firearms, using a two-tone Ford Fairlane. But then, that's a newspaper-reported event and not a bread-and-butter, daily occurrence in Bophelong.

The assegai was an unwieldy battlefield weapon, probably akin to a medieval knight's battle ax. Not that battlefield situations had ceased to exist in semi-urbanized Bophelong. No, not by a long measure. Battlefield-type encounters between armed and organized hordes of Basothos and Xhosas, or, for that matter, competing factions of each group, were still a frightening possibility. Such encounters were exacerbated by complex factors.

In traditional societies, adolescents and young adults are required to show proof of manhood. Individuals often showed such proof by killing marauding beasts. Proof of manhood in the absence of marauding beasts was often established by an evolving custom of spectacular fighting achievements. For achievements to be authenticated, however, they had to be widely witnessed. Consequently, leaders of competing fighting groups would select the day, hour, and venue for the armed encounters. The venues chosen would have to be: first, adequate enough to accommodate the expected spectators—mostly women and children—and second, the venue would have to offer an unimpeded view of the battlefield—otherwise how could the women authenticate the outcome? From their vantage site, the women would fan the flames of anger and ferocity by emotional ululations.

An additional factor that seemed to lead to large group fights was the presence of a South African institution deemed most instrumental in breeding black-on-black trouble: large migrant compounds in the immediate vicinity of black locations. At the entrance to Bophelong, the first, most conspicuous feature is the presence of a huge migrant labor compound. The migrant workers were shipped en masse from neighboring territories, especially Basotholand, and the areas designated by apartheid to be exclusively black tribal territories, the so-called Bantustans, were almost all located at the farthest outreaches of the country and were all extremely underdeveloped—otherwise how could they be sources of cheap labor?

Bophelong residents estimated that more than half of the local compound dwellers were either from Basotholand or from the Xhosa tribal reserve of the Transkei in the eastern Cape Province. It was natural for those from Basotholand to cling together as they faced the challenges of the new life in apartheid South Africa. The same was true of the others. It's an extremely small step to move from clinging together to face the challenges of a new environment to functioning as an armed, terrorizing gang. One factor that most likely played a key role in this attitude was the absence of women and children in the compounds.

The compound dwellers were indisputably traditionalists and

chauvinists who were exasperated by having to do chores that had traditionally been performed by women and children after they returned from work. Most would say extreme exasperation is a breeding ground for violence. Was it any surprise then that the compound dwellers were sometimes seen as bloodthirsty? Could the deprivation of a normal, healthy, family-oriented sex life have exacerbated the situation?

Since the migrant compound dwellers had been introduced into the area by white-owned business conglomerates, they were highly amenable to manipulation by the white-owned business and governmental power structures, including the police and the armed forces. It is widely believed in the Vaal Triangle that the police and the armed forces were behind some of the most savage brutalities of the last years of the apartheid era.

In preparation for battle, the weapons would be painted, sharpened, or reshaped as deemed necessary by the compound dwellers. Beyond weaponry, the more particular Basotho combatants would shave and Vaseline their scalps until they glistened. Why? It was simple; if anyone is going to cut my skull, it's better if my scalp is clean shaven so there's no danger of hair being trapped in coagulating blood, with all its implications of painful removal under the hands of clinic nursing aides.

The battle would start on schedule, amidst the ululations of the women, and continue until the victorious side had scattered and decimated its opponents. In the heat of battle, the Basotho would be singularly merciless; they would, for example, clobber a fallen foe harder under the pretence that the foe is not fallen but searching for stones! Sensing victory, the Basotho would break into song and poetry in praise of their lineage and nation—a scary and moving sight to behold!

When the battle lines exploded, the supposed forces of law and order would be discreetly absent in order to give the blacks enough time to reduce their formidable numbers. In the twilight of battle, they would appear with planned, dramatic suddenness. They would jump with practiced precision from the running boards on their fast-moving police vans to apprehend a token number of blacks, lest an "unfriendly" international press accuse a divinely ordained administration of barbarous indiscretions. Formal battles were, however, never a weekly occurrence. Their explosions were still stunning surprises. Though surprises, these battles seem to have been understood by the fellow tribesmen and spectators.

Attuned to the formalities of formal battles, adults were often at a loss when confronted by the brutality of routine Bophelong life. Their answer to these apartheid-generated acts of violence was often a shocking return to the days of yore in the form of organized, large-scale attacks against "modern, disrespectful" youth.

Bophelong changed its focus under the impact of the Pan African Congress' intensified campaign to confront apartheid. Instead of reeling under multifaceted violence inflicted by gangsters and tribal compound dwellers, the township was now reeling under the Pan Africanists' campaigns against the hated apartheid status quo. In the Vaal Triangle, Bophelong was not the flagship of the anti-apartheid effort led by the Pan Africanists. That flagship status belonged to the older community of Sharpeville. It was from Sharpeville that Nyakane Tsolo—unrelated to Phae—and the PAC's launching of the struggle was, in the first quarter of 1960, to send shock waves that were to permanently derail apartheid.

The PAC had called on the people of Sharpeville, regardless of political affiliation, to mount South Africa's biggest protest demonstration against the apartheid system. On the designated day, all Sharpeville residents joined the PAC leadership outside Sharpeville's police station, demanding an end to apartheid in general and an immediate cessation of some of apartheid's barbarous practices, including forcing all adults at all times to carry identity documents with them that contained extensive personal data including their place of residence and job status. Any adult black person found without a current, endorsed identity document was subject to arrest and imprisonment.

The peaceful Sharpeville anti-apartheid demonstrators were soon confronted by South Africa's modern, Western-equipped military firepower, and before long hundreds were either dead or injured. For the first time, a major South African anti-apartheid demonstration made headline news throughout the world.

The Sharpeville Massacre was followed by the banning of the two major black political organizations in the forefront of the anti-apartheid struggle. These were the Pan African Congress (PAC) and the African National Congress (ANC). The leadership of both organizations ended up in detention or exile. Quite a few members of the leadership and followers of all major anti-apartheid forces ended up seeking political asylum, initially in the neighboring countries of Lesotho, Swaziland, and Bechuanaland (now Botswana). From these neighboring countries, the exiled freedom fighters, among others, found their way to the African states of Tanganyika (now Tanzania) in the east, Ghana in the west, and Libya in the north. Of those who went overseas, some ended up in the Soviet Union and China, where they received, among other skills, instruction on flying sophisticated fighter aircraft. Most received mixed training in military and civilian skills before they returned as determined freedom fighters.

Most of those who ended up in the United States were granted comprehensive scholarships for study in universities scattered along the east coast. The impact of the Sharpeville massacre on the students of Pius XII College was immediate. An air of excitement and expectation impregnated the intellectual atmosphere on campus like no other event ever did, before or after.

In the midst of the post-Sharpeville Massacre excitement, Phae and some of the students decided to organize a Pius XII College branch of the Pan African Congress (PAC). Phae was elected chairman of the local branch. Since the PAC constitution specified that all chairpersons of recognized branches were automatically part of the party's executive committee, Phae found himself suddenly participating at the highest level of political activism—a move that posed the first major threat to the pursuit of the promise that had been the beacon of his academic life. In the midst of the spectacularly heated political developments of 1960s, the threat was not clear. The excitement of being part of a dynamic political movement overrode everything else.

With the aftershocks of massive liberation and political developments all over the African continent, students' lives at Pius XII College changed dramatically. From then on, students were obsessed with political developments anywhere on the African continent, from the Cape to Cairo and from Morocco to Madagascar.

Suddenly, students who had radios—and they numbered only a handful—became popular centers of attraction whenever it was time for world news, either from the BBC or the SABC (South African Broadcast Corporation). During world news broadcasts, probably more than ninety percent of the male students were glued to the handful of radios at the most popular news times, especially 1 and 7 PM Monday through Friday. Possessing a radio suddenly became a significant status symbol and a magnet that would attract listeners regardless of seniority or country of origin.

Needless to say, no one on campus owned a television set during this pivotal year. In fact, to Phae's knowledge, no one in all of southern Africa owned a TV set at that time. The repressive, white-dominated governments seemed to fear the liberalizing power of TV news coverage. In the absence of TV, radio news assumed a more tantalizing effect on listeners. Radio reports on developments in Ghana, for example, evoked images among listeners that turned out to have been more colorful and more intriguing pictures of Kwame Nkrumah-led, Africa-wide developments. In the absence of videos, the mention of developments in Accra, the capital city of Ghana, evoked images of a city that was bigger and more progressive than Accra at that stage could ever have been.

Caught in the whirl of exciting developments, Phae diversified his interests to accommodate a changing world. He started going to Maseru to attend PAC executive committee meetings and soon was comfortable in his new position of political prominence—member of the national executive committee of the Pan African Congress and chairman of the Pius XII university college branch.

Being an executive member of the second largest liberation movement in South Africa was a definite social boost for Phae. With increased political activism within Lesotho, Phae's realistic fears that he might be targeted by the South African Secret Service led him to investigate possibilities of gaining Lesotho citizenship—citizenship that made one simultaneously a citizen of the United Kingdom and the British Commonwealth of Nations.

Phae soon discovered a loophole in the British laws that could facilitate his acquisition of this new citizenship. In 1960, the British Commonwealth of Nations allowed anyone who could prove twelve months of continuous residence in a British colony or protectorate to apply for citizenship if he had the recommendation of significant members of the community. Phae knew that he had significant members of the community ready to support him. There were the academic heavyweights led by Dick Stevens on one side, and the spiritual leaders led by the Reverend Father McCarthy on the other. The only missing link was a member of the local Basotho community—a local chief, for example.

The need to have the backing of the local chief on his citizenship application defined one of the condition amelioration routes—frequent visits to the city Mafefs generally and, more specifically, visits with the local chief. Soon the chief knew as much about Phae as Phae deemed prudent and politically functional.

Visits with the local chief and villagers had many unintended consequences. First, the chief loved entertainment augmented by a glass or two of either whiskey or brandy. Phae was no stranger to either, though the amounts he used to consume from his father's servings were miniscule. In the company of the chief, Phae and his small group consumed an entire bottle per session—usually on a Saturday evening. With increased alcohol consumption, Phae found himself tempted to smoke cigarettes, not because his friends were smokers (and most were), but because he thought smoking would give him a more baritone voice. It didn't, and he had to go through the agony of quitting six months later—a move one of his new Johannesburg-bred friends, Alfred Moleah, used as a teaser.

"Phae," Alfred would say, "why are you quitting smoking 'ngoana mobu' (son of the soil)? You disappoint me. You sometimes behave too appropriately for your age.

"To put it bluntly," he would conclude, "you behave like an old man."

Phae did not object to Alfred's blunt remarks. He knew, and had always known, that his social behaviors would never be endorsed by the big city sleeks—a category of students sharing one thing in common: birth or long residence in a big city like Johannesburg, Cape Town, Durban, or Salisbury. Phae would typically respond to comments like these with outright laughter, a response that the city sleeks least expected and could rarely counter effectively.

Phae never told Alfred or any of his new contacts his true reason for quitting smoking: that he had found that he was running out of breath too quickly when exercising to keep fit. Phae would never tolerate any behavior he deemed dangerous or dysfunctional to his health. The divide between him and Alfred on this and similar issues outlasted their Pius XII days and continued even in their years in exile in the United States, where Alfred became a Temple University professor, and even much later when Alfred became a post-apartheid South African ambassador in Vienna, Austria.

Phae and his new friends soon made visits to the local village of Mafefoane—they all called it "city Mafefs"—routine. Monday to Friday were devoted to academic pursuits, but weekends, especially Saturdays, were earmarked specifically for outings, usually to "city Mafefs."

After Phae and his followers established a Pan African Congress branch at Pius XII University College, some weekends were spent attending political activism meetings in Maseru. Since the latter were irregular, the more dependable pattern remained the "city Mafefs" visits.

Some visits to "city Mafefs" did, unfortunately, turn out to be disastrous. During one of these, Phae and his entourage arrived at the village and went to a familiar house that was known for better service and a wider selection of alcoholic beverages. After entering the liquor-serving home, Phae's entourage noticed a Mosotho man sitting in the same living room with them. After greeting the man, Phae's gang continued discussing a BBC news item on United Nations' efforts to pressure South Africa toward liberalizing its apartheid regime. Since Phae's entourage cut across Southern Africa's diverse language groups, the accepted language for communication in all social settings was English, a fact neither Phae nor any of the members of his entourage ever questioned.

On this day, however, there was this inflexible Mosotho man who was voicing a determined objection to the use of English in a Lesotho household. Phae and his friends tried to ignore him, but the man became more assertive—even aggressive. Alfred signaled, surprisingly, to Phae that this Mosotho man had to go. Herman Makola, Alfred's best friend and a typical Johannesburg city-bred strong man, should, by all calculations, have been assigned this mission by Alfred.

Phae got up, moved to where the man was sitting, and told him: "If you can't accept our need to use English in our discussion, you are welcome to leave. Only a few of us here have any fluency in Sesotho, and therefore the use of Sesotho is out of the question. Furthermore, English is the second official language of Lesotho."

The Mosotho man, however, was unimpressed and uncompromising. Phae knew that trouble was inevitable. He issued the man a final order to leave, and when the man refused he literally tore him out of his comfortable chair and marched him toward the door. The man resisted, and Phae pushed him out. The man must have thrown a punch at Phae, who blocked it easily while he unceremoniously dragged the man outside.

As soon as the man was gone, everybody heaved a sigh of relief. It was soon back to the bottle and the discussions. These, unfortunately, did not last long. Within thirty minutes the Mosotho man was back with a following of armed Basothos. As soon as Phae and the others saw the invaders, they did what instinct ordered: run. In seconds they had disappeared into the darkness of the Roma mountains. They all slowly found their way back to the dorm with bruised bodies and egos.

At Sunday Mass the following day, Phae dutifully confessed to the priest in the confessional the "city Mafefs" misadventure. The priest listened carefully and at the end of the confession congratulated Phae for a thorough confession before blessing him. Phae exited the confessional relieved, though uncertain, as to what sin he and the others had actually committed.

Chapter 9

Feeling settled and more understanding of his social, educational, and extracurricular life, Phae began to focus on a minor but crucial aspect of his growth: his need for circumcision, a need that had been identified but never addressed by his father and his social-interactions coach at Kilnerton, Oupa. After circumcision, orthodoxy maintained, he would be free to seek a life partner. It was out of the question for him to approach this from the traditional route; there was no way he could or would devote weeks to the traditional rites of maturation in isolated, mountainous settings.

His circumcision had to be done in a recognized hospital that used tested and approved routines. After making some inquiries, Phae chose the Maseru hospital for the procedure. What was significant about his visit and short stay at the hospital was not the hospital's indisputable attention to quality procedures, but the fact that Phae fell in love with a nurse who was in attendance throughout the procedures! No outcome could have surprised Phae more.

The affair, unfortunately, had a short life span. Phae had more on his plate than he could handle! Worse, the nurse was stationed in Maseru, which was nineteen dusty, pothole-dotted miles away from Pius XII College! Before parting with the nurse, though, Phae made sure that she had a taste of the bodily instrument she had helped to fine tune. She was not disappointed during that erotic experience.

The physician who performed the circumcision interested Phae. Before performing the procedure, he had questioned Phae regarding his reasons for opting for circumcision. In all the years in which the physician, who was English by birth, had been at the Maseru hospital, he had never seen a university student or graduate request the procedure.

"Why?" he asked Phae, "did you opt for this procedure?"

Phae, rather surprised, asked in return, "Why do you ask?"

"Curiosity," the physician replied, unexpectedly adding, "Reports from the UK suggest that South African scientists are secretly working on experiments to use sexually transmitted disease to reduce the South African black population. I thought, as a university of Pius XII advanced student, you might have heard about it and are now taking the necessary preventive measures."

"Unfortunately no," Phae replied. "I've never heard of that, but I'm not surprised that the apartheid monster in its last attempts at survival would resort to that. I hope their experiments fail as much as has their ideology."

Years later, when HIV-AIDS was hammering at South African blacks' life expectancy, Phae recalled this conversation with disbelief.

The academic life at Pius XII University College couldn't have been tailored more to Phae's liking. He loved his majors: English and Modern European History. His English professor was a middle-aged, gray-haired man the students called Jimmy. Not only did Jimmy love his subject, but he was often so emotionally involved that he would sweep Phae along with him. Jimmy was mesmerized by what he termed "spontaneous creativity" in the works of certain writers, especially T. S. Eliot. Whenever Jimmy detected "spontaneous creativity," he would wax lyrical and become excited—an aspect of his lectures that Phae and some of the others found absolutely fascinating. At the end of one of Jimmy's classes, the students would gather and joyfully review the lecture.

Dick and some family members of the U.S. staff at Pius XII University College enjoying the Lesotho landscape. Note use of traditional Lesotho's hats.

Phae thought that most sections of modern world history lectures were interesting but uninspired until he was exposed in-depth to the story of the American colonies' struggle for independence, a struggle that, as Phae saw it, climaxed in the writing and publication of what he viewed as one of the consummate documents in the history of mankind: the American Declaration of Independence. This document mesmerized Phae. In brief but vivid language, it expressed the justification for armed uprisings against oppressive regimes. Within days of his exposure to the document, he had committed it to memory. Whenever and wherever opportunity offered, Phae would recite it like a call-to-arms. Needless to say, the American staff on campus soon assumed a new role in Phae's and his friends' perspective: they were a living, tangible, inspiration grounded in liberal ideology in the struggle against apartheid.

It is not clear by what mechanism word did filter down to the Americans on the university college staff that the students now viewed them as living, dynamic inspirations in their struggle against apartheid. Suffice it to say, it was not long after that that one of the American staff offered to give the PAC branch members on campus training in handling firearms! That the staff person, Ed Muth, was white and a family man with wife, Pat, and two kids was revelatory of the depth to which this small group of Americans had been committed to the anti-apartheid struggle. Ed Muth's weapons instructions were carried out inside a donga that was located not too far from the campus. Dick Stevens, who had no training in firearms—remember, he was raised to be a Catholic priest—chose a mixed bag of strategies as his contribution to the anti-apartheid struggle: writing letters to American congressmen and the White House informing them of the evils of apartheid and seeking scholarship money for those in need or likely to qualify for study abroad. Dick also published a variety of basically anti-apartheid studies in pro-African journals.

Dick Stevens's contributions in the struggle against apartheid took other, unforeseen forms. The most daring was assisting refugees in Lesotho escape to Bechuanaland. This was a one-shot affair given the risks associated with it. It was made possible by the fact that an American Peace Corps-type[1] volunteer assigned to the government of Basotholand was entitled to the use of a government-registered Land Rover. During one of the semester breaks, Dick and his Peace Corps friend decided to use the Land Rover to transport a full load of refugees across the vast stretch of treacherous, spy-infested, well-policed South African territory. That they succeeded was as much an act of merciful divine intervention as it was due to the naïveté of the Americans.

Had they been caught, what could have been the consequences? Their faith in the South African police's respect for the Basotholand government license plates, whether real or imagined, must have been the key to their having accomplished their mission. The only irony in this escapade is that Phae never saw Dick receive a thank-you note from the escapees. Suspecting that something must have gone wrong, both Dick and Phae promised to visit Bechuanaland in the near future to investigate.

---

1   The author remains uncertain about the exact status of this individual. He had, however, all the visible characteristics associated with Peace Corps volunteers then operating in Africa.

A less-risky intervention that Dick was associated with is also worth mentioning. He volunteered to deliver inspirational speeches to the students of the newly founded pro-apartheid University of the North at Turfloop, designated by apartheid for defined tribal groups only. Dick would give speeches not so much intended to warn the students against being used as instruments of apartheid now or in the future—most of the students already knew of that—but to give them more in-depth insights into the role of liberalism in the history of mankind in general and its possible role in the anti-apartheid struggle.

To provide for his safety while traveling to and from Turfloop in the northern Transvaal, Phae provided Dick with a loaded pistol that Phae hoped Dick would never have to use. Why? First, Dick, who had been brought up to be a Catholic priest, had never been taught how to use firearms. Secondly, and maybe more relevantly, the pistol contained only one bullet, and that one bullet was not the recommended size for the machine. Phae, barred from access to ammunition by apartheid, had to use tape to make the bullet fit!

Dick's best contribution, though, may have been through the letters he was writing to, among others, the congressional leadership in Washington D.C., the White House, and other supportive movements, wherever they might be. Dick's efforts in this area bore fruit when several qualifying Pius XII graduates—Phae included—were granted, throughout the sixties, an all-inclusive scholarship by the U.S. State Department to study in American universities. Another successful source of assistance for South African students that Dick tapped were student movements in the Scandinavian countries; the latter were soon offering Pius XII College students a wide variety of financial assistance and scholarships.

The beneficiaries of Dick Stevens's initiatives achieved almost unprecedented levels of success wherever they were placed. A good example of the success that these students could achieve could be seen in the achievements of Alfred Moleah. After earning a PhD from Temple University in Philadelphia, Pennsylvania, he joined the African Studies program there and remained in this capacity until he was invited to join a post-apartheid university in South Africa in a senior administrative role. Before leaving for South Africa, however, he had his PhD dissertation—detailing Namibia's struggle for independence—

published. Phae's autographed copy had the revealing message: "To my brother, Don Tsolo, with friendship, love, and respect."

After a few years in post-apartheid South Africa, the new ANC government appointed Alfred Moleah South Africa's ambassador to Eastern Europe based in Vienna. Dick Stevens had the supreme pleasure of visiting with Alfred's family during his tenure in Vienna. During those visits, the two immensely enjoyed reviewing the astonishing successes that a small group of devoted Americans who had been based at a small Catholic university in a tiny mountainous kingdom in Lesotho had achieved in making a significant contribution to the fight against apartheid.

This, unfortunately, is too far ahead in Phae's story. To rejoin Phae's story in its proper context, we need to backpedal to Pius XII College in the 1960s.

The female component of the Pius XII University College student body was in many ways an indicator of the low enrollment of women in the educational institutions of Africa south of the Sahara. The total number of registered women never exceeded the thirties during Phae's years at Pius XII University College. While the census data was significant, what was intriguing to Phae was the visibly conservative social orientation of the female students. During the years from 1960–62, not a single girl smoked cigarettes on campus—at least definitely not in public—even though these times predated the anti-tobacco campaigns. The girl who tore the Catholic campus out of its female conservatism was a Johannesburg beauty who enrolled in Pius XII College in the 1960s. Her name will forever remain in the history books regarding women's liberation in the Roma valley.

When Phae first saw Barbara Masekela pop her cigarette pack out of her handbag, gently ease out one cigarette, and sensuously light it not too far from the food center, he was stunned! "Who was this incredibly brave and daring girl?" Phae, who was then an assistant lecturer at Pius XII after having graduated in 1962, asked himself. Not only was her smoking daring, it was done in the style of a contemporary, Hollywood movie actress! Her high heels and colorful outfit made her total appearance as dazzling as Phae had ever seen. Barbara had other assets, which she soon revealed. She could tango like no girl Phae had ever seen, outside Latino dance films. On the dance floor during a

Phae's University College of Pius XII on graduation day, with Barbara Masekela,
"a one-woman social revolutionary machine."

typical Pius XII student social, Dido and Barbara would never miss the chance to dance together to a hit tango tune.

Watching them glide across that floor was like a dream come true. Barbara, people soon conceded, was a one-woman social revolutionary machine.

In her grasp for social status, she soon had Phae caught in her amorous embrace. The affair, though, was short-lived; Barbara needed somebody higher than an assistant lecturer to satisfy her insatiable appetite for social success. Her next victim was the white American Peace Corps-type whose government Land Rover had, with Dick Stevens' help, transported refugees to Bechuanaland. Before long, these two had eloped to the United States.

Unfortunately for Barbara, that affair couldn't have lasted long either. During a mid-1960s trip to West Africa, Phae was alerted to her presence in a nearby hospital as a long-term patient. Phae visited her but did not have the guts to ask key questions. Is that why, decades later, while stationed in Washington D.C. as South Africa's ambassador to the United States, Barbara would never invite Phae to any of the socials at the embassy, to which the public, including Phae's longtime friend, Dick Stevens, was frequently invited? Or was Dick invited because he was white? Did that also explain why Barbara never assisted Phae in regaining his South African citizenship, even after years of trying while residing in the United States? It was strange what contradictory, lingering aftereffects apartheid could have!

For Phae, graduation from Pius XII College in record time was never in doubt. His meticulous dedication to the promise he had made from his early teen years assured him of praiseworthy success. Upon his graduation, the college invited him to join the staff as an assistant lecturer. Phae gladly accepted the invitation. Before he could take up his position, though, he undertook the most politically dangerous move of his college years: knocking the black Rhodesians down from their monopoly of the executive positions of the Pius XII University College student union.

How had the Rhodesians acquired these positions? They had undiluted, raw political ambitions that were more intense than those of similar groups from south of the Sahara. Also important, they were more likely to be financed by deep pockets. Because Rhodesians had better scholarships with liberal personal-expenditure allowances, the Rhodesians began teasing South African male students with statements like, "When we take the South African girls on a date, we do it only in the interest of feeding the poor masses!" Statements like these forced Phae to play a significant role in toppling the Rhodesians from their citadel.

To topple the Rhodesians constitutionally, however, Phae and his co-conspirators had to convene a general meeting of the entire student body. The Pius XII University Student Union constitution unfortunately required that before a meeting of the student body could be convened, those convening the meeting would have to set out in clear language the reasons for the meeting and simultaneously submit the motions to be raised during the meeting. Phae and his co-conspirators—Joel Moitse, a South African self-professed Marxist; Timothy Zwane, Phae's roommate from Swaziland; and Bob Hira, the only Indian student from Natal—had to come up with a strategy that would allow the Rhodesians, in their capacity as executive leaders of the student representative council, to convene the student body meeting while accepting its strict requirements.

Phae designed the strategy to circumvent the union's constitutional safeguards. The first step was to write a letter to the president of the student union alerting him to the low morale of the student body when it came to crucial student union matters and the obvious need to discuss this in an open meeting of the student body without preconditions. Since there was an article in the constitution requiring motions to be submitted in advance for regular meetings, Phae suggested that to facilitate this extraordinary meeting, the article requiring the advance publication of motions be suspended. Joel Moitse fine-tuned the language of the request, and within days the Rhodesians, led by Edison Zvobgo, were in agreement and approved the convening of a major student union meeting without written motions submitted in advance.

When the meeting started, Joel Moitse led the charge. The current student union executive, he claimed, had failed to detect the profound dissatisfaction that existed in the student body due to the attitudes of the Rhodesian executives who had condescending attitudes toward their fellow, non-Rhodesian students who did not have liberal scholarships. After the presentations, Phae moved for the adoption of a motion arising from the discussions: a vote of no confidence in the current student body executives. If the student body adopted this motion, the Rhodesians would be forced out of their positions and new officers would be elected. The adoption of the motion would, indisputably, be a local coup.

The student body enthusiastically voted for the motion of no confidence in the present executives, thus administering the first coup in the history of the Pius XII University College student union. Edison and his crew resigned reluctantly. They never regained control of the Pius XII College student union. Phae was elected the new student union president, with Timothy Zwane as the vice-president.

Toppling the Rhodesians was Phae's major nonacademic achievement while at Pius XII. As student union president, he was obligated to attend international student union conferences, gaining influence beyond any he had ever imagined. It was as president of the Pius XII University College Student Union that he toured West African educational institutions in the 1960s. It was during one of these tours that he met Barbara Masekela in a West African hospital.

After his BA graduation in 1962, Phae enrolled in a postgraduate correspondence history course with the University of South Africa. His focus was South Africa during the founding years of Jan Van Riebeck's governance soon after the Dutch landed near Cape Town in 1652. Why this period? Phae passionately needed to understand how apartheid had evolved. It was only while doing postgraduate BA honors work in South African history that Phae found new and enlightening material on this subject, including the exciting finding that the ancestors of the Afrikaner not only did not believe in apartheid but thought, as did the leader of the mission, Jan Van Riebeck, that a racial mixture between black and white produced a qualitatively better specimen of humanity!

Phae made another history-related discovery while at Pius XII. He visited the historic mountain fortress of Thaba Bosiu where the Basothos had inflicted a decisive victory over the Boers in the nineteenth century. The reason for the visit was simple: to witness the crowning of a new king for the kingdom of Lesotho. This king was no ordinary run-of-the-mill king; he was educated at Oxford. Not only did Phae convince his American friend and political science lecturer, Richard Paul Stevens, PhD (Georgetown), to go with him to the ceremony but also to go using the traditional Sesotho means of transportation to such occasions—on horseback. Dick, never the one to shy away from an opportunity for adventure, assured Phae that he was more than ready for the trip.

On the coronation day, Phae and Dick left on rented horses early in the morning to give themselves local travel flexibility. The horseback trip was slower than expected; neither Phae nor Dick were comfortable, let alone adventurous, on rented horses' backs. It was upon arrival at Thaba Bosiu that Phae noticed something highly unusual about Dick's pants: they were dripping blood! The friction from the saddle had rubbed away all of the skin covering his bottoms! Clearly the man had most likely never been on horseback for more than a few minutes before. This experience was one of the foundation stones upon which a solid and lasting friendship between Dick and Phae was cemented.

With Dick Stevens's mobility highly compromised, a thorough investigation of the features that made Thaba Bosiu an impenetrable fortress was limited. In spite of this limitation, the two discovered a secret long known to the Basothos; the Basothos had been able to inflict several defeats upon the rifle-armed Afrikaner attackers because there was only one narrow corridor that invaders could use to access the fortress. All who attempted to access the fortress were killed in that narrow corridor with amazing ease! Furthermore, the flat mountaintop could sustain hundreds of people, including their livestock, indefinitely.

Dick during motorcycling exercises in preparation for tour of southern and central Africa.

Chapter 10

Within less than a year after the Thaba Bosiu episode, Dick and Phae, now sharing a house in the lecturers' quarters of the campus after Phae had been offered a position as a South African history assistant lecturer, planned to undertake a groundbreaking tour of central Africa using a second-hand Lambretta scooter that Dick had bought from a dealer in Pretoria, South Africa. This obviously dangerous safari fortunately never was undertaken; the scooter fell apart before reaching Maseru—a mere nineteen miles away. The Italian makers of the scooter could never have anticipated its use under Basotholand road conditions! After repairs, the scooter was donated to the Timothy Zwane-backed Swaziland progressive political party.

The failure of the Lambretta-inspired safari did not, however, kill the idea of a Phae and Dick safari tour of central and maybe even eastern Africa. A Cuban-born black American, H. George Henry, head of the economics department, heard of the idea through a third party. He mentioned his interest to Dick. Dick welcomed the opportunity, especially since George owned a Bloemfontein-purchased, brand-new VW buggy. Moreover, George's wife, Lynne, an American east-coast black with an incredible sense of humor, was in agreement.

With that final detail in place, the four took off on a warm sunny day. The safari route, vaguely planned, required traveling through apartheid South Africa to Swaziland—a dicey proposal given the racial composition of the buggy's occupants: Phae, black, South African-born, and traveling, for the first time in his life, on a British Commonwealth of Nations passport; Dick, white, Pennsylvania-born, with anti-apartheid sentiments as strong as any you will ever encounter, traveling on a U.S. passport;

H. George Henry, portrait.

and George and Lynne, both black and American, using, as far as Phae knew, U.S. passports.

The trip across South Africa to Swaziland was uneventful. The VW buggy and its cargo did not, surprisingly, draw much attention—even from law enforcement. Expecting a warm welcome in the British protectorate of Swaziland, the buggy's occupants received their first reality shock: hotels in Swaziland did not cater to racially mixed guests!

The manager of the hotel they were booked at was uncompromising; his hotel did not provide overnight accommodations to racially mixed groups. When Dick first heard this he exploded—a behavior that no one in the traveling group had ever seen displayed by Dick, who had been brought up to be a Catholic priest and was prevented from achieving the same by health considerations. Completely unprepared, Dick, firmly believing that British colonial laws could not sanction segregation in the protectorates, threatened to report the manager to the local police. The manager was unimpressed; he knew the Swazi version of British Commonwealth laws. Dick and his entourage stormed out of the hotel on a sacred crusade: to report the actions of the hotel management to the police and to hopefully file charges.

A "green" but ill-advised "bathroom" stop inside the Kruger National Park.
An elephant is in far background

When the VW buggy charged out of the hotel parking lot, anger-riddled Dick was the driver for the first time during the trip. Given Dick's anger, level-headed George's driving would have been way too slow. Dick found his way to the nearby Swazi police station, where they found out, to their surprise, that the local police station was staffed by white police who pretended not to know what Dick was complaining about! "Had the hotel manager called the police in advance?" Phae wondered. Dick and the entourage soon learned that trying to get Swazi police involved in conflicts between mixed racial groups and segregationist hotel management was tedious and exasperating.

With all these complications, the buggy's occupants decided to minimize their stay in Swaziland, so they limited their visit to witnessing only one event: a sacred, traditional ceremony wherein the chief of the Swazi nation annually chose a new bride from among his virginal subjects. After the spectacular but morally repulsive ceremony, they went back into South Africa en route to Southern Rhodesia via the Kruger National Park, the second designated stop on their safari. This time the drive was more northward and took less than six hours.

At the gates to the Kruger National Park, the buggy's occupants were warned while paying their park entry fee to stay in the car, as this was dangerous territory. Again, the racial composition of the buggy's occupants did not attract obvious attention.

The only other question from the gate attendant was one no one had prepared for: "Does anyone in the car have a firearm?" For a split second no one reacted. Phae, probably unbeknownst to the others, had a firearm in his traveling case. He hesitated but then said loud and clear: "Actually, I do!"

Phae reached for his traveling case and pulled out a revolver. The gate attendant took the firearm's details and then handed it back to Phae. The entire transaction was surreal: never in his life had Phae ever thought he would admit to a white South African authority figure that he had a gun! He had never heard of a black South African being legally entitled to a firearm! But then, he remembered, he was no longer a typical black South African. He was now under the protection of the British Commonwealth of Nations, even though the Swaziland authorities did not seem to realize the legal implications of that status.

The drive through the Kruger National Park was exciting; neither Phae nor any of the buggy's other occupants had ever seen the concentrated collection of wild animals they were now seeing all over the park. One collection, however, tempted Phae to make a special request. It was a herd of elephants grazing. They looked, at one and the same time, powerful, peaceful, and graceful.

"Can we please take photos of the elephants?" Phae requested after they had just passed them.

No one in the buggy could possibly have been against taking photos of elephants, but Phae's next request seemed to challenge the Park guidelines; Phae wanted to take photos of elephants while they were doing something dramatic, not while they were gracefully grazing. Without explaining—if he even knew what he meant by "something dramatic"—he asked George to reverse the buggy closer to where the elephants were grazing. George stopped the car and hesitated for a split second when he realized he didn't quite remember how to get the VW into reverse. After a few trials, he succeeded. Dick provided the camera. The buggy reversed slowly toward the elephants. When they were near enough for Phae to exit the car to take the pictures, George stopped the car without changing gears and simply kept the clutch depressed; the efficient VW motor maintained a low, unintrusive, idling rumble.

The elephants remained indifferent. Phae took a few shots and then realized that proximity alone did not guarantee dramatic postures. He needed a dramatic shot or two. He could not figure out a method to get the elephants in a dramatic pose, and Dick wasn't much help.

Out of the blue, Phae settled on a method that instinct told him would give the desired result: He screamed in a loud, piercing voice. The elephants flapped their huge ears and then began charging toward the intruders. Phae managed to take one or two dramatic pictures before jumping into the VW buggy, followed closely by Dick. Both hoped that George would take off and drive away from the elephants as soon as they were in the car. George, as expected, stepped on the gas pedal while simultaneously lifting his foot off the clutch, and the car sped backwards toward the charging elephants! There was instantaneous panic in the car, in the middle of which George's hands landed on the car horn, and the buggy let off a frightening, piercing yelp. The charging elephants stopped in surprise, giving George the crucial seconds needed to change gears and get the car out of harm's way. Never before or since were the buggy's occupants closer to certain death! It was left to Lynne to turn a near tragedy into humor.

"George, for goodness sakes," she said. "You almost killed us! I told you the day you bought this car that you bought a pack of problems. Now, there you are in the middle of the Kruger National Park with the world's biggest animals in hot pursuit! And what do you do? Instead of driving away from the charging giants, you reverse right toward them!

"George," she continued, "though you may never admit it, it is this car to blame. For starters, each time you change into reverse, you have to pull the gear toward you." Here, Lynne made an unmistakably overdramatized demonstration of George's pulling of the stick shift. The demonstration sparked instant laughter—a needed ingredient in the present context.

"Then," Lynne said, continuing her theatrics, "you push it to the side before depressing it downwards! After depressing the stick shift, you have to slowly lift your foot from the clutch to let the car move forward ..." Lynne managed to demonstrate each of the demanding steps involved in the process while evoking continuous giggles.

"Lynne, aren't you exaggerating the steps involved in changing this car's gears?" George protested timidly.

"Oh, no! I am not," she replied. "You should have bought yourself a regular American car without those complicated gear shifts," Lynne concluded, as Dick drew their attention to colorful giraffes stretching their long necks to grasp the young, juicy, leafy shoots of a huge tree.

"And what are those running away from us?" Phae asked. "Over there where there appears to be a savanna patch!" Phae pointed toward springboks leaping away in the distance.

"They are springboks," Dick answered, using a park guidebook to identify the animals. "I like them," he continued, "they remind me of deer back in Pennsylvania."

Before anyone could reply, their attention was drawn to a new development. A road sign read: "Slow down, you are approaching Beit Bridge," which is one of the few official entry points to Southern Rhodesia from South Africa.

Arriving in Southern Rhodesia exposed the group to another surprise: integration, or its look-alike, propagandized version partnership, was far from being a reality. After clearing border-crossing facilities, the VW, now en route to Salisbury, the capital city of Southern Rhodesia, started exceeding the speed limits of the Kruger National Park as George was becoming more familiar with his German-made auto. Within minutes of crossing the border, Dick spotted a roadside hotel and restaurant. They decided to stop there for their first taste of the food products from the widely advertised partnership between races in the new Rhodesia.

Dick led the group into the hotel's restaurant with his face full of positive expectations. As they entered the restaurant, a huge, fat-looking, Afrikaner-type woman emerged from behind a cash counter. Her first words were a stunner. "Stop!" she ordered the group. Turning to Dick she inquired pugnaciously, "Who are those?" pointing a fat finger toward Dick's companions. "They are not allowed in here," she said explicitly. Dick was furious. An apartheid-type encounter with an obese Afrikaner woman was the last thing he was expecting in a British colony that the media touted loudly as a "partnership"—a new flagship of colonial liberalism. Dick knew with pristine certainty all that propaganda could not have been successful without a basis in fact.

His Africa Digest readings had quoted several partnership enactments. In fact, in his briefcase were several articles explaining the applications of "partnership" in Southern Rhodesia.

"If you don't know that the new partnership is law, I will be glad to show you extracts of relevant ..." Dick was not given the chance to finish his sentence.

The angry, obese, Afrikaner-type woman interrupted him with a bold declaration.

"If you are not out of the restaurant and hotel in the next five minutes, I am going to get my husband to shoot you bastards out of here," she concluded, reaching for a wall-mounted telephone with Calvinistic self-assurance and arrogance.

In that crucial moment Dick's radicalization was completed. Suddenly the shades of priesthood were transformed into a powerful anger, not only against the obese Afrikaner in front of him but also against the entire colonial propaganda machinery that had deceived him. From that moment, Phae knew that the Dick Stevens he had known was now gone—blown away by thoughtless reactionaries, leaving a hardened, determined reformist. What remained of the old Dick Stevens was a fighting machine determined to face colonial racists without compromise at any level. Realizing what was happening, George and Lynne pulled Phae to the side and whispered, "We have to cool Dick." Phae nodded approval but still had to wrestle with some aspects of the current developments.

For starters, the rawness of the Afrikaner-type white woman's anger and the vehemence of her tone were unlike anything anyone in Phae's entourage had ever encountered. These were the kinds of behaviors that the news media that was broadcast through the BBC in Lesotho had insinuated were nonexistent in this British territory on the verge of self-governance. What could have gone wrong? How could so many well-educated travelers misjudge the reality behind the partnership touted far and wide?

Fortunately for the safari seekers, they all realized one crucial fact: they were judging the situation by city standards, forgetting that they were far from the big cities! It was a truism long established in Southern Africa: cities are oases of liberalism. Rural areas were and would always be for the foreseeable future conservative. Once this fact had been accepted, an air of relief descended upon the VW's occupants. With regained faith, they steered the VW toward Salisbury, the capital city. Their assumption that big city life would be different from rural or small town ultraconservatism proved to be mercifully well-founded. The liberalism and racial tolerance of Salisbury was manifest wherever they stopped for gas or for snacks.

Even in the city's biggest hotel the atmosphere of partnership—meaning the absence of apartheid-type restrictions against racially mixed interactions—was evident. The social matrix of Salisbury was diametrically unlike what they had encountered soon after crossing the border. In Salisbury, partnership, it appeared, was a living, dynamic fact of daily life.

After Salisbury, the group visited the historic Zimbabwe ruins—the most famous relics of a structure of unparalleled significance. While at the ruins, one couldn't help but feel that this part of central Africa must have been at one time the industrial-commercial hub of a thriving economy that likely had connections to the Middle East and Asia.

The defense potential of the ancient city reminded Phae of Thaba Bosiu. Could the mindset that converted Thaba Bosiu into an impenetrable fortress have had historic links with the Zimbabwe ruins? Was it to the Zimbabwe fortress that Tshaka, the famous king of the Zulus in what is now the Natal province of South Africa, went to seek technological assistance in converting Zulu spearheads into metal shafts? "Most unlikely," Phae silently admitted, but the thought was conceptually intriguing.

While traversing Southern Rhodesia, the buggy passengers were impressed by the vastness of the white-owned commercial farming enterprises. Two crops seemed to dominate the economy: corn and tobacco. Cattle were the predominant livestock. To George, the economist, there was absolutely no doubt that these farming operations met or probably exceeded some of the strictest performance indicators usually used to assess the performance of emerging economies. Some of the sprawling farms boasted their own landing strips and hangars for small aircraft!

In the far north, Southern Rhodesia is bordered by Northern Rhodesia. The border was sharply defined by the Zambezi River. It was to the Zambezi that Phae most looked forward to going, especially to that small section of it known as the Victoria Falls. The falls were and are known to be so beautiful and fascinating that when seeing them, one understands without much explanation why a nineteenth-century British explorer and the falls' assumed first white visitor, Dr. David Livingstone, thought they were so beautiful that God's angels must have beheld them in their flights! Was it any surprise then that some people called the Victoria Falls one of the wonders of the world?

The Pius XII entourage crossed into Northern Rhodesia, soon to be called Zambia, at the colorful Victoria Falls Bridge. Entry into Northern Rhodesia was easy, especially since passport requirements were often waived for travelers entering from Southern Rhodesia. Phae liked Northern Rhodesia. Here racial tensions were significantly ameliorated or absent. People of all racial descriptions seemed warm and welcoming. All of the towns, from Livingstone near the Victoria Falls to the capital city of Lusaka and beyond to the Copperbelt, had character and charm. None had South African-type squatter compounds or cheaply constructed locations. All the towns were relatively medium-sized and newer.

The political tone of Northern Rhodesia was inspired and nuanced by the liberation leader Kenneth Kaunda, a Pan Africanist and nationalist. As a nationalist, Kaunda impressed Phae then, and as he had always done through the media, by his efforts to define the essence of what it was to be African. At the heart of being African, Kaunda frequently preached, was devotion to African humanism: the belief that our best actions came from tapping the aspects of God in all of us and respecting the positives in our African heritage.

As a Pan Africanist, Kaunda warmly welcomed fellow freedom fighters from all over Africa—an attitude that underlay his approval of the construction and subsequent operation of Africa's first top refugee school near Kabwe. The school, to be financed and staffed by Americans, would be called the Nkumbi International College.

The idea of an international refugee school in the middle of Northern Rhodesia fascinated Phae. For the first time, Phae saw an opportunity to fight apartheid outside the framework of Maseru exile party politics, even though those had given him an opportunity to contribute to the struggle at an ostensibly elevated level as a member of the national executive committee of the Pan African Congress. Phae made a decision while viewing the Northern Rhodesian landscape from the confines of the VW buggy: "If the Americans were ever to construct that school, I would be the first to apply for a teaching position there."

Before the '60s were over, Phae delivered on that promise and decision.

In the comfort of the Lusaka Hotel, Dick made a suggestion that changed the composition and destinations of the VW buggy entourage. The suggestion was made soon after supper while the entourage was viewing the exhibitions of traditional crafts that lined the Lusaka Hotel's corridors.

"Guys," Dick began, "we have had an incredibly productive safari. I have seen countries I never imagined I would ever see and had near-death encounters with elephants I never thought remotely possible. I have seen the incredible Zimbabwe ruins with their compelling suggestion that there is more to the history of southern Africa and southern-African institutions than any of the literature I have seen has ever suggested. George and Lynne have been more than generous throughout this trip. Without their VW buggy, this trip would never have materialized. With their buggy and their insatiable sense of humor, we have really had a wonderful time. Now, however, I think it's time we reassess our safari. Should we go on to East Africa?"

When Phae heard the word "reassess," he immediately became suspicious. Dick, he figured, must be up to some tricks. George was equally taken aback and responded in a style typically his, asking, "What do you mean?"

Lynne, visibly happy with developments so far, opinioned, "Dick has had enough. You know, George, how political science types think. Dick has seen enough samples of political developments south of the equator and now figures it's time we returned to the cool heights of tranquil Basotholand so he can start work on articles to any one of the many pro-Africa magazines he writes for."

"Oh, Lynne, please stop it!" Dick appealed. "I do not think I fit any 'political science type.' To be honest, I think it's prudent that we truly assess the possibilities, given the fact that we have the time, of taking in the huge expanses of East Africa. Quite frankly, I would be the last to suggest going that far and over terrain that uncertain and in a car not fully equipped for the purpose. What do you think, Don?"

Phae was caught by surprise. He hesitated and then dropped a bombshell. "Dick, I have truly enjoyed this safari so far. It has met and exceeded all my expectations. I am far from exhausted and, frankly, I feel I am more than ready to cross into East Africa. That said, I would like to suggest that we part company here. George and Lynne and the VW buggy should, preferably, return home. I know that it would be excruciatingly painful to part with them for a week or two, but I strongly feel that asking them to drive into East Africa on unpaved and relatively untried road surfaces with limited or nonexistent emergency services would be asking too much.

"Worse, Dick," Phae suggested, "we are three guys with one woman in foreign lands. Don't you think Lynne might be having unrevealed ordeals that may only get worse with more intensified exposure to more challenging safari conditions?"

Phae's presentation, slow, deliberate, and carefully nuanced, seemed to have tilted the scales in favor of a split: the Henrys were to return to Basotholand, and Dick and Phae were to continue into East Africa. The next day, George and Lynne were on their way south. Dick and Phae opted to travel to East Africa via Malawi, previously called Nyasaland.

Accessibility and acceptable road conditions helped decide the mode of travel to Malawi—buses and taxis. The Malawi visit was brief but exciting, and in many ways an eye-opener to authentic and traditional African lifestyles. The people of Malawi were warm, out-reaching, and extremely helpful. Their patience when explaining directions was impressive and meticulous.

The people in Malawi were not particularly fazed by meeting a young, black, South African man in the company of a white man. To have said that Dick was American to the Malawians would not have made much sense; it was sufficient that he was white and not a racist. With nonstop help from the Malawians, Phae and Dick soon found accommodations at a small inn along the country's huge Lake Malawi—a lake that Phae, at first sighting, assumed was an inland sea. The staff at the inn was warm, courteous, and extremely helpful. Once Phae and Dick had settled in, they were served hot English tea in their room; how often could you find that service offered without additional cost? After tea, a member of the staff volunteered to show them sites along the lake that were deemed safe for swimming. The need for caution emanated from a recent incident; a crocodile was recently seen sunbathing only yards from the inn, near the spot where a tributary river joined the lake.

Without giving much thought to the dangers of encountering crocodiles, Dick and Phae soon found their way to the lake and enjoyed some relaxing swimming on that hot, sunbathed day. After swimming, the two decided, most unfortunately, to nap on the lake's white sandy beach. When they woke up hours later, disaster had struck; Dick's skin was badly blistered! Without skin protection against ultraviolet sun rays, his skin was more vulnerable. It took days before Dick's condition was back to normal. By then, unfortunately, it was time to leave for East Africa.

Booking a flight on the small passenger planes that connected central Africa to East Africa was simple. You simply walked to the airport, bought your ticket, and without much ado walked to the plane parked on the tarmac. There was minimal fanfare at the airport. Security, if it did exist, was far from visible. There were no crews to welcome you aboard, and definitely none to serve you in-flight snacks.

Phae, years later, swore that the plane was also far from being air-conditioned. The plane windows, he claimed, were wide open throughout the entire flight! The flight was otherwise uneventful, and the landing at Dar-es-Salaam unremarkable. After landing, the pair had to walk from the plane, unable to hide from the airport's exceedingly high coastal temperatures and scorching sun.

The Dar-es-Salaam Airport was virtually empty on the day of their arrival. Only a handful of staff was present to process their landing and passport formalities. There were no customs-related questions asked. For both Phae and Dick, visa requirements seemed to have posed no problems at all, and within minutes after their arrival, the two were bargaining with a local taxi driver for a ride to the nearest decent hotel.

The taxi ride was short; clearly the driver did not take advantage of the fact that they did not know the name of a hotel or its location in the city. The taxi driver chose the hotel for them! The fee charged for the trip was so minimal that both Dick and Phae opted to double the tip. The taxi man was delighted. Unfortunately, there were no practical means to re-establish easy contact with him were they to need his services in the near future.

After a brief rest, Phae gave Dick's fragile skin a good rubbing with suntan lotion. He couldn't afford to take any more cheap chances with his friend's sensitivities to the piercing rays of Africa's equatorial sun. The two fell in love with Dar-es-Salaam almost instantaneously and spent the rest of their first day along Dar's beautiful beach.

It was not long before Phae spotted, for the first time in his life, a whale wallowing peacefully in the quiet waters of the Indian Ocean. His excitement at the sighting was spontaneous and electric. In seconds, his excitement with his discovery had ignited waves of curious gossip along the beach. To all and sundry it was obvious that Phae was not and could not be a local, especially since he was accompanied by a white man. Phae soon found out East Africans rarely suppressed their curiosity. Within minutes, curious beach patrons surrounded Phae and Dick.

It soon became clear that most of these were no ordinary beach-loving patrons. They were recent converts to Julius Nyerere's revolutionary African socialism who were determined to assist all Africans suffering under white minority rule. Language was no major barrier; almost everyone spoke English with a fluency that was impressive. They soon had ascertained Phae's standing on the vital questions regarding Pan Africanism and Tanzania's obligations toward, among others, exile movements fighting colonialism and apartheid anywhere on the continent, which was consistent with theirs.

Soon Dick and Phae were whisked off on a tour of the city by the excited new contacts. Of the places they visited, few stood out. One that did stand out was the Tanzanian President's residence. Phae literally walked up to the door unchallenged—an experience he had cause to recall years later when he tried to take a picture of Mandela's home in an upper-crust Johannesburg neighborhood and was ordered by the guards—practically at gunpoint—to not stop to take pictures of the former president's residence; South Africa's post-apartheid security barred such indiscretions!

The next significant stop was at a refugee compound just outside of town. While the accommodations looked basic, Phae was impressed by the neatness and tidiness of the place, which was a prime indicator of the priority that Tanzania assigned to the continent-wide liberation struggle. When Phae left the compound, he had the uneasy feeling that he was destined to revisit the place in one capacity or another—more likely as a conduit of confidential transactions between the Dar-es-Salaam and Maseru PAC offices.

Another site that Phae and Dick visited while in Tanzania was Zanzibar, an island a few miles off the coast. Phae could never forget that visit. The island's population appeared to be Muslim and Arabic, and everything about the place—the architecture, the layout of the small towns—had a strangely non-Southern African appearance and vibe. The men and women dressed differently. The shopping centers and their frequently scented merchandise seemed unlike anything Phae had ever seen before. The exotic and the disturbing were exacerbated by the repulsive images evoked by the sight of the island's historic sites. These had been preserved, reportedly to remind the world of the sad to barbarically cruel role that Zanzibar had played in the abhorrent slave trade.

It was from this island and these historic slave-detention and shipment sites that slaves from the mainland were shipped to wherever the market forces of the time dictated. Favorite markets were as far away as the southern states in America and, prior to the abolition of the slave trade in the British Empire, many of its scattered colonies. Phae felt revulsion when he realized that he had stepped on one of the major sites behind the black Diaspora.

Phae could only take so much of the historic negatives evoked by the slave-trading historic facilities before bolting out. Quite clearly, his Pan-Africanism had not figured out and accommodated the role of Arabs in the history of Africa. Before returning to the mainland, Phae sought spiritual cleansing. He had to rid his body of the conflicting and unsettling images imprinted in his innermost psyche by the sight of the slave-trade historic sites. A cleansing source, mercifully, was readily available: the warm, enchanting waters of the Tanzanian Indian Ocean coast.

It took only minutes before Dick and Phae were waterborne. Phae had never swum in deep sea water before. Here, he discovered a secret he never knew: it's easier to swim in deep seawater than it is to swim in rivers or pools. Seawater supports you, and you do not need to overexert yourself to stay afloat! With that pleasant discovery, he swam almost half a mile away to a floating platform conveniently provided by the government.

Dick, on the other hand, was always, by his admission, an excellent swimmer. Knowing that Dick was within calling distance in case of an emergency gave Phae the needed external support to bolster his adventurous spirit.

Beyond Tanzania the two visited Kenya, starting on the east coast. The east coast of Kenya was charming. One or two villages had U.S. coins that had once been used, some suggest, as currency. Now they adorned coastal women's ears!

From the coast, they boarded a train with stops in Nairobi and the Ugandan capital of Kampala. The train ride within Kenya was characterized by one unforgettable fact for Phae—it was a steep climb all the way to Nairobi and beyond. Because it was a steep climb, the coal-fired engine labored more markedly and gave off a little more particle–filled smoke than was comfortable for somebody who liked to keep his train windows wide open.

To both Dick and Phae's surprise, Nairobi was a fairly large contemporary city. The people were reasonably accommodating, maybe even friendly. None of those whom Dick and Phae met in Nairobi exhibited any political radicalism or significant support for Pan African institutions and movements. None showed any unusual reaction when introduced to a South African black man. Quite clearly these Kenyans were enigmatic. Unfortunately, deciphering enigmas was not one of Phae's obsessions during this trip. So off to Kampala the two went aboard another coal-fired steam engine train. This section of the trip, it turned out, had the most dramatically scenic landscapes of the entire safari.

Beyond Nairobi going to Kampala, the landscape is one of Africa's most gorgeous. Going through it was one of the few times that Phae regretted not having a movie camera to capture some of the stunning land formations. Sighting the marker of the equator was an irresistible photo-op. Their arrival in Uganda was a culmination of surprises, and Kampala itself was the biggest surprise of all. From the moment he stepped off the train, Phae knew he was in an unusually beautiful country with greenery, lakes, and stunning mountain views.

Everywhere he looked there were signs of intensive commercial agriculture nestled side-by-side with indigenous botanical beauty. Abundant everywhere were exhibits of nature's generosity with equatorial and tropical fruits of all descriptions growing with impressive vitality.

It was from Uganda, Phae was told, that one of the world's most important rivers, the Nile, originated. As if in testimony to this, Uganda boasted some lakes that were so huge that Phae thought, at first seeing them, that they were extensions of the Indian Ocean! Their pristine and apparently unpolluted waters dotted with fishing boats were inviting. In the far distance across the lakes one could see, in misty outline, the contours of the bordering mountains.

Instead of staying in a hotel, Dick suggested that it would be more cost-effective if the two could be guests of a local Catholic center of worship or monastery. It didn't take long to find one. It was located in the far western part of the country, with a view of the striking mountains defining the western edges of Uganda. The two shared a comfortably sized room with two windows facing a nicely landscaped garden. As guests of the monastery, Dick and Phae had main meals in the same cafeteria as the priests. The menu was simple but tasty and well-presented. Coffee and desserts were excellent and homegrown. Bananas and several other tropical and equatorial fruits were served throughout the day to the guests, the residents, and the staff.

Using the monastery as a base, Dick and Phae visited several sites of interest, including the famous university of Makerere, the parliamentary buildings, the East African equator marker, and, more significantly, Kampala's largest mosque. The two decided to make the visit to the large mosque a special visit, and clearly a first for Phae. The visit to the mosque was made, for Phae, unforgettable by the fact that visitors were required to take off their shoes before entry.

Evenings in the surrounds of Kampala were spent, unpredictably, in deepening the relationship between Phae and Dick. The two had ample time in the evenings to sit down and acquaint each other with significant aspects of their past. Dick, a scholar with a passion for detail, often set the tone of the discussions. During one session, Dick asked Phae a question that few ever asked regarding Phae's view of his elementary school days following the family's move into Bophelong in December of 1950.

"Don," Dick started, always preferring to call Phae by the shortened version of his European name—remember, all black South African youth of the era had "European names" in addition to their traditional African names—"I am not clear about your elementary school days in Bophelong and your teacher training year in 1959. Do you mind telling me some of the features of those years from whatever angle you prefer?"

Phae gave Dick one of those looks that said loud and clear, "You asked for it!"

"Dick," Phae began, "my elementary school days are and will always be unforgettable. I recall them with incredible clarity. All of my elementary school teachers were black, urbanized South Africans. They loved their work, and the community rewarded them by giving them the highest recognizable status in Bophelong's social circles.

"In the Bophelong area in those days, to be a teacher meant one had achieved the highest academic and social standing in the community. It was assumed without question that teachers were 'highly' educated and were, therefore, automatically superior models for all to follow. That I have subsequently discovered that some of what they taught as facts were not so, and that even some English language spellings and pronunciations were unfortunately incorrect does not diminish my underlying respect and admiration for them.

"There was," Phae continued, "for example, teacher Pooe, who was fresh out of college and eager to uplift the educational standards of the until-recently rural communities of Bophelong. These communities were, up to the time of the foundation of the location in the late 1940s, still rooted in superstitions, ancestor worship, and other related rituals all characterized by one overriding trend—use of nonresearch-backed explanations of disease causation. Similarly, curative interventions were not research-based."

"Are you talking about witch doctors?" Dick asked, adding, "There are students at Pius XII University College who are still fearful when traveling inside Lesotho that some traditional medicine advocates might identify them as ideal candidates for ritual murder."

Phae hesitated before responding. "I hate to disappoint you, Dick," he said. "You can count me as one of those. I have heard too many true tales of ritual murders not to be careful when out in the villages, especially at night."

"I'm sorry to hear that, especially since you love your Saturdays at City-Mafefs," Dick responded.

"Thanks!" Phae answered warmly. "I know you do not interpret fear and concern as belief. I obviously and indisputably do not believe in witchcraft or the use of uncontrolled traditional cures. Further, Pan Africanism and its advocacy of respect for African culture and traditions does not mean the acceptance of witchcraft. Pan Africanism respects and advocates the use of scientific methodologies wherever and whenever applicable. And," he continued, "it would be a sad day in South Africa when a reputable national leader would advocate the contrary."

"Amen!" Dick responded, signaling Phae to return to his life story.

Phae, alert to Dick's cue, returned to his main theme. "Teacher Pooe's love of tennis played a not insignificant role in my love for the sport," Phae explained. "I well remember the days when he would turn up at the Bophelong tennis courts in his white tennis outfit and use only balls from newly opened cans, with the audible sound of the opening of the can witnessed by the other players. To me that was, and still continues to be, the height of a tennis player's attention to detail and sophistication!

"Another unforgettable, young, sport-loving teacher was teacher Ramokgopa," Phae continued. "He was also a boxer with an orthodox boxing style emphasizing speed and accuracy over power. His impressive moves in the ring, reminiscent of Ali's 'float like a butterfly and sting like a bee' style, had spectators frequently yelling with admiration. That I was both a boxer and a tennis player interacting recreationally with my teachers in the gym and the tennis courts was a great moral booster and helped cement my love for both sports.

"The other unforgettable weakness of my elementary school

teachers," Phae continued, adopting a tone with reduced enthusiasm, "beside whippings with rulers, was highlighted during my last month in elementary school. We were being briefed on course options beyond elementary—an incredibly important session in the transition from elementary to secondary. A key teacher undertook that mission with enthusiasm but failed hopelessly to clarify to the students what mathematics was all about. He failed to show the connection or relationship between arithmetic, a subject taught in elementary schools, and mathematics, taught in post-elementary schools. When asked what the differences were, the teacher kept saying that in mathematics, symbols were used more often than numbers. When asked why symbols were used instead of numbers, he choked and dismissed the class! Because of that teacher's failure, I never did a mathematics course even though I was the best-performing arithmetic student of my elementary school years. Isn't that informative?" Phae concluded. Dick nodded sadly in agreement.

"Other unforgettable shortcomings cropped up during English poetry classes," Phae continued. "My primary school teachers taught me poems dealing with daffodils and nightingales when they had no clue what those looked like! That having being said, there is one positive characteristic I remember them for: their unrelenting enthusiasm for their subjects and their students!"

During 2004, years after the downfall of apartheid, Phae had cause to recall this aspect of the teaching staff at the elementary school in Bophelong he used to attend. He telephoned the then current principal from his brother's home in Sebokeng, a few miles north of Bophelong, to ask if the principal could confirm his having studied there in the 1950s—a fact that, if confirmed, could have facilitated Phae's attempt to regaining his South African citizenship. The principal's response was a surprising, "Absolutely no! There were no records of those years left in the principal's office!"

"Thanks," Phae calmly replied. "I'm not surprised. You are not the only South African institution to have lost, or misplaced, important documents. The Ministry of Home Affairs in Pretoria has achieved a chilling notoriety in document misplacement or loss. Rumor has it that up to six percent of the South African population is currently without proper ID documents thanks to Home Affairs' appalling handling of public documents and records. Reports reaching the U.S. consulate in New York suggest that they are being investigated."

In conclusion, Phae asked the principal, "Can I quote you on this in the future?"

The principal, in obvious panic, pleaded, "Please, no! Don't ever quote me on that topic!"

Phae, surprised, replied passionately, "How could a principal of a South African school in the days after apartheid be afraid of being quoted on such a simple subject? It's not your fault that apartheid did not provide you with the document-storing facilities that could have enabled you to store those documents!"

At this point, Gemmina, Phae's brother's wife, who had introduced Phae to the principal, gave Phae a nod while saying, "Brother, let's stop there!" And with that nod, a revealing unrehearsed remark by a school principal, it cast a pall to end an innocent but nevertheless controversy-generating verbal exchange.

Dick and Phae visit the equatorial marker in East Africa

Phae enjoying the Ugandan landscape

Soon it was time to bid equatorial Uganda good-bye. On the last day, just before leaving the guest room they had occupied during their stay, Dick and Phae decided to bid the priests and monastery staff good-bye. For reasons neither could rationalize, they decided tacitly to do this separately. Dick went first, and when he returned, he immediately took his traveling bags out of the room. When it was Phae's turn to go and bid the priests good-bye, he made sure his wallet and passport were safely stored in the traveling case he left in the room and that the windows to the room were tightly closed since rainfall here was frequent and sustained. The entry door to the room was, however, left closed but not locked.

When Phae returned to the room to pick up his luggage after the farewell rituals with the priests, he noticed, with surprise, that the window opening to the backyard was ajar! He knew for certain that he had made sure the windows were closed before he left to bid the priests good-bye. A strange instinct compelled him to look outside the window. What he saw shocked him. On the manicured lawn, his wallet and passport were scattered like somebody had thrown them out in a hurry.

Phae was momentarily shocked beyond words. He immediately went to the backyard, picked up his wallet and passport, and then thanked God almighty for saving him at a crucial time. Had he lost his passport and wallet in the heart of East Africa, how would he have had another reissued? And over what time frame? How would he have managed financially in the interim?

Phae, regrettably, opted not to report the incident to either the police or the priests, though one fact stood out in bold relief: Phae had interrupted a theft. The perpetrator must have heard Phae's footsteps returning to the guest room from bidding the priests farewell. Since escaping through the door leading to the main corridor would have exposed the culprit easily to Phae as he walked along the main corridor to the room, jumping through the rear window into the backyard was the best escape route for the culprit. The wallet and passport must have fallen out of his pockets as he jumped out of the window and landed on the lawn. The thief probably had not realized that valuable items had fallen out of his pockets and had simply kept running into Uganda's impenetrable, entangled, equatorial growths.

The incident marred probably the most exciting part of the entire safari. Following the break-in, Phae decided to return to Basotholand as soon as possible. He was lucky to book a flight from Nairobi to Johannesburg the following day. From Johannesburg, he would use the train to Maseru with a brief stopover in Bophelong to visit with his parents.

Dick, on the other hand, chose to widen his safari to include a visit to the headline-making, newly independent states of Ghana and Nigeria. Phae gave him a warm hug and reminded him of the need to be extremely careful during his West African travels.

Dick had cause to remember Phae's words when a Lagos hotel staff tried to hook him up with prostitutes—acts that shook Dick, a man brought up to be a Catholic priest, profoundly. In outraged moral protest, Dick charged downstairs to the hotel manager's office to protest the acts of the hotel staff.

The manager could not believe that Dick would object to his staff's efforts to make his stay at the hotel steeped in sexual pleasure! The manager promised, in spite of his disbelief, to honor Dick's concerns; no prostitutes were sent to Dick's room that night!

Unfortunately, that did not assure Dick a good night's sleep.

Throughout the night, he could hear with incredible explicity, numerous amorous performances in the adjacent room!

Before that night was over, Dick had decided to shorten his West African sojourn. Within days he was aboard a British Airlines passenger plane en route to Maseru via Johannesburg. Before departing, Dick sent Phae a telegram, addressed in care of Phae's father, Bantu Cafe, P.O. Bophelong, Republic of South Africa, advising Phae of his expected day and time of arrival at Johannesburg's Jan Smuts Airport and of his availability for an overnight visit with Phae's family. Replies were to be sent in care of British Airways, Jan Smuts Airport, and Johannesburg, where Dick would pick them up upon his arrival.

Phae, having stopped at Bophelong on his way to Lesotho, was impressed and surprised by Dick's daring initiative. Had he forgotten that this was apartheid South Africa and that whites were not allowed in black townships for social visits? With incredible daring, Phae informed the Bophelong administration of Dick's expected visit without saying anything about the visitor's color. Incredibly, no one in the Bophelong location office detected the oversight.

Phae tried to find a rationale for Dick's suggestion.

The logistics of geography and economics made Dick's suggestion sensible. In the 1960s, Lesotho was not connected to the world by commercial passenger airliners. All international tourists had to disembark in Johannesburg. From Johannesburg they could go to Maseru via Phae's preferred route: train.

In extremely rare circumstances, some would charter small planes from Johannesburg's international airport to Maseru, where travelers landed on non-tarmac strips with not a single building or any airport security in sight! Upon arrival, passengers depended upon friends or private contacts to pick them up; Maseru landing strips were not serviced by any public transportation system. Not unlike the Maseru bus terminus, the landing strips offered no bathroom facilities of any kind whatsoever. Worse, in case nature made demands, the land was barren; there were no trees or boulders to give one cover.

What about immigration and customs formalities? The government of the British Protectorate did not think that this was applicable to airborne arrivals!

To arrive in Johannesburg after a long flight from Lagos, Nigeria, and to fly from Johannesburg to an airport of this description in Maseru, Lesotho, was clearly too much for Dick. Common sense dictated that he should take Phae's favorite mode of transportation between the two cities: trains. And since trains passed near Bophelong, where Dick suspected Phae would stop before going to Maseru, why not join Phae in Bophelong?

The two would then travel "together" by train to Maseru via Bloemfontein. It was so simple and affordable, Dick must have thought.

On the designated day and time, Phae picked up Dick at the Vereeniging train station with a visibly controlled show of intimacy. Why "visibly controlled"? Warmth between blacks and whites in the Vereeniging of the 1960s was virtually nonexistent. In this context, a public display of innocent love and intimacy between the two would most likely ignite police suspicion, if not lead to outright arrest. The two, accompanied by Phae's friend, Sam Mokete Mosiea, drove quietly to Bophelong. They arrived in Bophelong after sunset. The guards at the gate failed to notice Dick's color and simply waved the car into the location. And with that simple act, they allowed the first white person to visit Bophelong for an overnight stay.

After arriving at Phae's family home in Bophelong's cul-de-sac known as Nhlapo Court, Dick was greeted with, again, guarded enthusiasm by Phae's family. Were the family to display their true enthusiasm, the attention of the immediate neighbors may have been attracted with unknown outcomes. Even though controlled, the enthusiasm was electric. Both Phae and Dick seemed to have been overwhelmed. Phae's mother—Lydia to Dick, but Ntlapu to the rest of the family and neighbors—managed to overcome the chaos of the welcome and made a long-awaited announcement: "Dinner is ready!"

The dinner announcement seemed to have caught Dick off guard. After the long trip he would, ideally, have preferred to have taken a shower and made a change of clothing before dinner. Not too sure of the appropriateness of his question, he chose to toss it at Phae. Its simplicity belied its nuances. "Where's the bathroom?" he inquired. Phae understood the source of Dick's caution. In Lesotho, typical traditional African homes did not have inside bathrooms, called in local parlance toilets, and frequently, they didn't have outside ones

Phae's permanent contribution to the Nhlapo Court cul-de-sac
A huge, gravity-defying poplar

either. The bushes and the boulders provided the necessary cover. If none were available, it was no problem. To the Basothos, a man's back suffices as a covering boulder!

Phae amusedly looked at Dick and whispered: "The bathroom is behind you." And sure enough, there was a door across the corridor leading to the boys' bedroom.

"I need to first check if it is in usable condition," Phae added as he walked into the bathroom.

Whoever designed the Bophelong houses knew how to build dependable bathroom and sewer systems. In all the years Phae had lived in Bophelong, the family had never had cause to call the plumbers for help! Even if the aesthetics of the system left a lot to be desired, its dependability was incredible, especially when Phae factored in the frequent use of newspapers for toilet paper!

Phae secretly checked for the presence of toilet paper in the bathroom and to his eternal surprise, someone had the foresight to make sure that on this day, with this visitor in mind, decent toilet paper had been provided! And, wait. Not only was there toilet paper, but other bourgeois bathroom provisions were clearly available as well, including a roll of colorful paper towels!

Phae proudly signaled Dick. "Come on in. Everything is all right!" Phae assured him.

Dick smiled when he saw the obvious joy in Phae's report, and in that insignificant moment, Dick knew instinctively that this short visit was going to be a success! He was not disappointed.

Dinner was spectacular. The meats included barbequed chicken and chunks of choice beef cuts, with vegetables aplenty, including Phae's favorite: beet-root laced with sliced onion steeped in vinegar. For dessert, Ntlapu served her favorite preserved peaches after asking Dick to do the honors of opening the air-proof canning jar. This finger-licking, tasty treat was Phae's favorite. While red and white wines were available, Phae's father, Jerry, who arrived during the dinner servings, offered his favorite brandy, which was served in a miniscule and fancy brandy glass.

Jerry could afford to be open and generous when serving European beverages. He was one of the extremely few blacks allowed by law to purchase and consume European—meaning white—alcoholic beverages. A sound system Phae had bought for the family before his departure provided unobtrusive classic jazz music in the background.

Looking outside the dining room, Dick could see Phae's permanent contribution to the Nhlapo Court cul-de-sac landscape: a huge, gravity-defying poplar on the edge of the lawn tearing away at the front fence. On this night, the cul-de-sac was well lit, thanks to the full moon and the streetlights, and it was mercifully empty of uninvited guests.

So much seemed to have silently conspired to give Dick the surprise of his life, and Phae's family an unintended opportunity to burst apartheid-fostered hatreds!

It was soon midnight and time for all to retire to their bedrooms. The equivalent of the master bedroom opened to the right side of Dick, who stood admiring the poplar from the center of the dining room. To the left was the bedroom for the girls: Pauline, who was the oldest; "Tsidi"—the abbreviation for 'Matseliso' or Elizabeth—who was the second born; Hoti, who was the third born; and the last born, 'Mina'—the most beloved of the Tsolo children. The boys' bedroom entrance faced the corridor connecting the dining room, kitchen, and bathroom. At its max, it accommodated four boys: Ben, who was the eldest; Phae, who was the next; followed by the frequently ill William; and the last born of the boys, Molupe, pronounced Modoopee.

Tonight the boys had to accommodate the approximately six-foot–tall, white American visitor, Dick. Lucky for everybody, Dick was gifted at improvisation. In seconds, he had figured out that capturing the dining-sitting room sleeper couch and towing it into the boys' bedroom was the magic cure for the sleeping dilemma. Within minutes, everybody was sound asleep in spite of the occasional snores.

Chapter 11

It was not until after 9 AM the next day, a Sunday, that Richard P. Stevens, PhD, of Georgetown University, Bophelong's first white overnight visitor, woke up. Probably unbeknownst to Dick, not only was apartheid South Africa racist to the extreme, it was also, in some ways, as snobbish as the English aristocracy. Not only was socializing with the working class for persons of his qualifications taboo, but when you compound that with the race issue, Dick's overnight stay should have been an utter impossibility.

Incredible as it may seem, Dick had managed to squeeze a few additional hours of quality sleep in an overcrowded bedroom on an improvised bed. As soon as he was up, Dick found his way to the bathroom. Along the corridor to the bathroom, he could hear distant conversational voices that were actually coming from the kitchen area. Dick paused, listened carefully, and, to his surprise, found that he could identify the voices, other than Phae's, that is.

In the bathroom, a small section of the medicine chest had his informal name written in clear letters. There was a brand-new shaving set next to a carefully folded towel and washcloth. "For crying out loud, they didn't have to do this!" Dick muttered to himself.

Ntlapu and Phae must have detected Dick's movements because by the time he left the bathroom breakfast was ready.

Phae was the first to greet him. "Good morning, Dick! It seems like you had a good sleep!" he said.

"You must be kidding!" Dick responded. "This is the best sleep I have had for weeks."

Phae was glad to hear Dick's response. He knew with a high degree of certainty that there was more truth than exaggeration or flattery in Dick's response.

"Mom will be glad to hear that," Phae responded, adding, "Dick, Mom is in the kitchen. Do you want to give her a Sunday morning hug?"

Dick smiled and immediately took steps toward the kitchen. As he entered the kitchen, Phae's mother, standing next to the indoor coal stove, seemed pleasantly surprised by the obvious joy written on Dick's face. Dick rushed to her and gave her a warm hug followed by a good morning kiss on the left cheek. Ntlapu must have been not only blithely surprised but ecstatic. This was the first kiss she had ever received from a white man. She blushed in unmitigated joy, adding, "Thank you. I have a surprise for you. Breakfast is ready!"

"Oh! That's awfully nice of you," Dick responded, adding, "I was hoping Don and I would fix you today's breakfast, but I guess my oversleeping took care of that!"

"No problem!" Phae's mom replied. "In my house and in my culture guests do not cook Sunday meals. You will have the chance, hopefully, to one day return the favor."

Breakfast was a South African hybrid. It included distinctly South African features: fried Boerewors/sausages, corn meal cooked to the consistency of a smoothie, and plenty of fruits and vegetables. The tea was also distinctly South African Rooibos. The more typically served Ceylon Tea was also available. Of interest to Dick, coffee was not offered, though he knew that if he had asked, coffee would have been prepared and served. Similarly, cold drinking water was not readily served.

Breakfast conversation was lively, made more so by the beautiful family pictures on the living-dining room walls. The biggest and clearly most expensive was an oval-shaped, framed enlargement, in color, of Jerry and Ntlapu, Phae's dad and mom. Evoking more discussion from

Dick was a picture in black-and-white of Phae in his boxing outfit and stance. Dick couldn't resist commenting.

"Don, that's you in your boxing days!" he exclaimed. "You haven't changed much. How old were you when that picture was taken?"

"Probably fifteen," Phae replied, adding, "I was then in the flyweight division."

Dick noticed a certificate that Phae had been awarded when he won the Northern Transvaal amateur flyweight championship in 1959 and asked, "Where were you when you won that award?"

"Boy!" Phae exclaimed, adding, "Dick, you're a genius at digging out historic facts. Anyhow, I was at a blacks-only—sorry, that's not correct—maybe more appropriately, a tribal teacher training college east of Pretoria, not far from Kilnerton. The college is closed now. Apartheid decreed it should be transferred farther away from white South Africa to a Northern Transvaal area called Turfloop where a tribal university was to be opened.

Phae in "his boxing outfit and stance."

"What precluded me from going there, in addition to my fervent desire to be at Pius XII University College," he explained, "was an incident which occurred during a history class discussion." Phae was in the full belief that Dick would ask for more information on the incident. Phae was not disappointed when Dick fired back, "Please explain!"

Dick was detecting a defining moment in Phae's stay at that buried institution. Phae did not hesitate in delivering a response. "The history lecturer was an Afrikaner who had just delivered an Afrikaner version of a white-black contact situation during the Afrikaner invasion of southern Africa. He wanted feedback from the students. No one bothered to answer. The Afrikaner lecturer exploded in fury, yelling, 'Answer, you sleeping dogs!'

"No sooner did the outrageous comment hit the ceiling than the students started packing their books for departure from the class and the Afrikaner racist. The students' spontaneity and the definitiveness of their response were stunning—even to themselves. The Afrikaner lecturer was fuming in anger but couldn't stop the stampede. That evening, the students convened a meeting of the student body, which was an easy task given its small size. The resolution from the student body was unambiguous: boycott the history classes. The boycott was total. At its height, I knew that my fate with apartheid educational institutions was sealed. Turfloop, where this Afrikaner history lecturer was scheduled to be the head of the history department, was no longer an option.

"After the weird incident, my determination to go to Pius XII University College increased a thousand fold.

"Before the end of the week I sent a telegram to the Pius XII University College administrative office, advising them of my definite intent to start studies there at the beginning of the 1960 academic year. A copy of the telegram was mailed to the Isaacson Foundation Fund in Johannesburg to make sure that the scholarship-funding source was updated.

"The Bantu Normal College, Dick, was an apartheid-era institution destined for an early demise. It had one of the smallest student populations—under two hundred. The composition of the student body was reflective of the apartheid ideology. All the students were black; not even coloreds were admitted!

"If Pius XII University College with a 400-plus student body had only thirty-five or so female students, can you imagine how far fewer females there were at the Bantu Normal College?" Phae asked, continuing without waiting for Dick's response. "You probably wouldn't be shocked to hear that even in that attenuated female student population, I fell in love with a girl whose integrity and sincerity and seriousness of purpose I will never forget. She was, I think, a Venda from the Northern Transvaal. Her name was Monica Netshilindi."

Here Phae paused, looked teasingly at Dick, and asked, "Does that name ring a bell?"

Dick hesitated before replying. "No! Should it?"

"Yes!" Phae shot back. "She's at Pius XII University College as we speak. She's quiet, self-effacing, and polite to a fault."

"Most interesting!" was all Dick could say.

"Most interesting!" Phae's mom echoed. "I never knew I was that close to getting a 'makoti' from the Northern Transvaal."

"A 'makoti,' Dick", explained Phae, "is a daughter-in-law. In African tradition and culture, the relationship between a 'makoti' and a mother-in-law is a special relationship that is carefully nurtured from the date of the engagement to at least the birth of the first child. That relationship deserves more than a chapter in the sociology and social work textbooks of the future South Africa. How that special relationship is nurtured determines to a large measure the relationships between immediate families."

Phae's mom, never one to be bogged down in speculation, brought the intellectuals down to reality. "You two!" she said. "Do not forget that your train for Lesotho leaves at 6:30 PM from the Vereeniging train station. You need to be at the station at least fifteen minutes before departure. It's now 11 AM, and Dick has not seen what there is to see of Bophelong," she concluded.

Phae's mom's implication that there was something for Dick to see in Bophelong took Phae by surprise. How do you organize a Bophelong sightseeing tour for a white American man whose legality in the location was extremely dubious? The answer, to Phae's mom, was simple: Dick was brought up to be a priest. He underwent the requisite training until illness precluded him from the priesthood without permanently disqualifying him. So, Dick could be touring Bophelong on this Sunday to assess the potential for a Catholic presence!

"Dick," Phae's mom cautioned, "the moment we leave this house on a tour of Bophelong, you are here to investigate the feasibility of establishing a Catholic presence. Whoever asks, the project is at such an elementary stage that you are in no position to reveal any details."

Dick burst out in laughter. Did she know he was brought up to be a Catholic priest? Phae's mom didn't concern her self with details, except the detail related to the need for an almost immediate departure on the sightseeing tour. Within fifteen minutes, they were all ready to leave on this unprecedented walking tour. Before leaving, Phae noticed a Bible in his mother's hands. "My mom," he muttered to himself, "isn't taking chances!"

The walking tour of Bophelong was surprisingly uneventful for Dick. For Phae and his mom, it was blissfully so. Why? All those who saw Dick walk with dignity in a black suit assumed he was a missionary. Intrigued, Dick sought clarification from Phae.

"The Afrikaner head of the Dutch Reformed Church visits about two times a year," Phae explained. "During his visits, he drives straight to the Dutch Reformed Church, and after service, he drives straight out. Whether alone or with his wife, he never drives anywhere beyond the confines of the Dutch Reformed Church. The only other whites I have seen in the township were Jews from Johannesburg who drove in to pick me up en route to a UNO-backed volunteer international work camp in Lesotho. In fact, those Jews were the only 'whites' I ever had an intelligent discussion with outside of white academia. I so loved that camping experience that I extended my stay to include the entire summer. By the way, Seodi Molema, from Mafikeng on the southern South Africa-Bechuanaland border, joined that camp for several weeks," Phae concluded.

"What project did you guys work on?" Dick asked, half-surprised by the rich diversity of Phae's experiences.

"The project was, in many ways, simple," Phae began. "We set out to provide a typical isolated Lesotho village with clean, clear, and cool running water from a mountain source. The UNO, most likely with some limited contributions from the British Basotholand protectorate government, provided the hardware: plastic pipes, faucets, et cetera. Luckily, not only was the project feasible, it was also sustainable— made so by the fact that many Basotho volunteer workers participated in digging the trenches for the pipes. Their participation assured sustainability from a maintenance angle. Pressure in the water system was provided by the location of the over two-hundred-and-fifty-gallon capacity reservoir on top of the mountain where the water source was located. The nature and altitude of the source assured the sustainability and dependability of the water supply. The altitude of the source also assured the system's continuous operation without the need for

Serenely studious Seodi Molema, Pius XII University College Ladies' dormitory

generated energy," Phae concluded. After glancing at Dick, he added the closing remark: "After completion, we monitored the system for two weeks before handing it over to the village management."

"Don!" Dick could not help exclaiming. "You are an incredible young man. You have really managed to puncture significant holes in the apartheid system without much fanfare."

Phae was genuinely surprised by Dick's reaction. Phae never deliberately perceived participation in international work camps and similar activities as puncturing holes in apartheid's armor. It never occurred to Phae that assisting the Basotho people in improving their standard of living by enabling them access to clean drinking water at their doorsteps was significant in the bigger context of southern African politics. It slowly dawned on Phae. An economically viable Basotholand meant lesser dependence on apartheid South Africa, and that economic viability includes the smallest steps toward betterment, steps such as a dependable and sustainable water supply system constructed with the active cooperation of locals. Quite clearly, small, local actions can have wider ramifications. Thinking along these lines tore Phae from the abstract to the concrete. "How will we get Dick safely out of Bophelong into the Vereeniging train station en route to Maseru this evening?" he wondered.

"Hell!" Phae whispered to himself. "I need to get us out of here as soon and as safely and quietly as possible."

An exit strategy soon crystallized. They would rent a taxi to the Vereeniging station with Dick still posing as a would-be priest seeking converts. Since both had prepurchased tickets, they would wait on the open platform where the parameters separating the whites from the nonwhites were ill-defined. When the train arrived, Dick would wait until he knew which coach Phae was assigned to. It would be infinitely easier for Dick to find Phae during the trip than for Phae to find Dick—apartheid is more forgiving of whites found in "non-European" coaches than of the reverse. The impressive coal-powered train arrived and departed on schedule. The overnight trip to Maseru was uneventful. Arrival in Maseru was early the next day. The longest section of the trip still awaited them—the nineteen-mile bus ride on pothole-riddled, dusty dirt roads with the bus making frequent unscheduled stops en route to the Roma Valley and Pius XII University College.

Chapter 12

Nineteen sixty-four was an epochal year for Phae. It was the year when Phae's new world collapsed in front of him with frightening rapidity.

The first major development began as a rumor. The Oblates were unable to raise enough funds in Canada to continue running the extremely progressive southern Africa Institution of Hope. It was rumored the Oblates were going to cede the ownership of the institution to the governments of the three British protectorates of Basotholand, Swaziland, and Bechuanaland.

All staff, unless they were specifically informed otherwise, would be terminated. Rumor rapidly turned into fact, and Phae's contract with the institution was terminated with minimum fanfare. The same fate awaited most of the other staff, including Dick and Dido Diseko—two of Phae's enduring friends.

Termination would have been an unmitigated disaster had Phae's contact from the international voluntary work camp days not turned into a savior. Charles Manyeli, a truck driver with the Basotholand Ministry of Local Government, offered Phae room and board. Phae was the second South African "refugee" to be accommodated in the Manyeli household. The first was a fascinating civil servant, Simon Phamotse, who was willing to share his room with Phae. The Manyeli family, with Simon's active help, made Phae's stay in Maseru after his contract was terminated smooth and culturally enriching.

With the support of Simon and the Manyeli family, Phae sought a job with the Basotholand British Protectorate Civil Service. Phae had all the qualifications for employment in the civil service—a BA from Pius XII University College, even though the actual certificate indicated that the University of South Africa in Pretoria had granted his certification. In addition, Phae had several years of teacher training and two years of assistant lectureship at Pius XII University College. Over and above the academic qualifications, Phae was a citizen of the British Commonwealth of Nations and a resident of Basotholand—a citizenship that was automatically transferred to Lesotho citizenship when the protectorate acquired political independence.

An advertisement in the local paper offered the first desirable position for Phae to apply for in the protectorate civil service. The position required a BA certification. Phae applied. Not only did he have a BA qualification, but he was currently enrolled in his second year of postgraduate diploma-seeking education. He had all the required qualifications, including what he thought was a trump card— his ancestors were Basothos!

For the job interview, Phae wore an expensive suit and beamed confidence. When he entered the interview room, he sensed an unexpected coldness from the interviewers that should have been a clue. The leader of the interview team did not mutter a welcoming comment. The first question from the interviewers taught Phae a regrettable and unforgettable lesson. The question was simple but pregnant with implications:

"Mr. Tsolo, where is your father?" The question caught Phae off guard. Not only was the question completely irrelevant, it was in extremely poor taste as an interview opener. Phae had tackled surprises before but never of this nature. He answered with a visible effort at remaining calm.

"My father, dear sir, is a proud Mosotho helping the people of Bophelong improve their plight under apartheid. He is chairman of the school board, a lead member of the location's board of control, and a highly respected member of the local church. He is the one who encouraged me to return to the land of my ancestors to make my contribution to the birth of a proud, independent, and viable Lesotho. Not only did I fulfill my father's wish by returning to the land of our ancestors, but I proudly took up Lesotho citizenship at the first opportunity. I can say to you here and now, I am proud to be a Mosotho."

The Mosotho interviewer was not impressed. His cold, almost calculated response betrayed his motive. "So, your father is still living in South Africa?" the interviewer asked. In that response from the interviewer, Phae learned an incredibly depressing lesson for a black, South-African-born Pan Africanist: there are not many people in the neighboring territories that were ready to welcome black South Africans running away from apartheid—especially when these runaways become qualified competitors in the labor market.

The interview ended without a single job-related question regarding qualifications or experience. Phae left the interview room disappointed and depressed beyond belief. This was the last and only vacancy he applied for in Basotholand. The corollary of the decision to cease applying for Basotholand job vacancies was the onset of a profound retreat from identification with the Basothos and their beautiful mountainous kingdom—an identification Nyakane had enhanced way back in his elementary schooling days.

The next job advertisement Phae responded to was from Northern Rhodesia—the future Zambia. The advertisement was for a secondary-school teaching position in social studies. Dido Diseko, Phae's friend who had been an assistant lecturer in the Pius XII Physics Department, had first seen the advertisement. Since he was applying for a similar position in a different Northern Rhodesia secondary school, he thought it would be nice for Phae to join him in that far away part of the world.

Dido's idea more than fascinated Phae. Phae had been to Northern Rhodesia and was an admirer of Kenneth Kaunda, the nationalist leader of the pro-independence movement in that country.

Phae submitted his application, and within two weeks he had an invitation for a job interview. He flew into Lusaka on a one-way ticket—due not to his being overly optimistic but following a carefully calculated plan. Whatever the outcome, he would return by train so that he could stop in Bechuanaland to double-check aspects of a report that

Elias Ntloedibe had submitted to the Pius XII Pan African Congress branch during Phae's Pius XII University College days. Ntloedibe was assumed to have been a dependable transmitter of information between branches and the executive offices in PAC's Maseru exile office.

Ntloedibe's report had claimed that he had seen a plane take off from Francistown with more than two-hundred-and-fifty PAC freedom fighters for training in West Africa. The report had intrigued Phae, whose knowledge of airports in the British protectorate countries was limited to the Maseru landing strip with a capacity limited to small private planes. A two-hundred-and-fifty-passenger plane, Phae reasoned, must be huge and therefore must require landing facilities more superior than those offered anywhere in Basotholand. He yearned to see an airport of this caliber in a country slated for independence in the near future. Travelling by train from Lusaka to Maseru would offer him a chance to see this airport at Francistown, Bechuanaland—a town on the railway route to Maseru. Needless to say, Phae found out later, both the airport and flight were nonexistent ideological Ntloedibe propaganda fictions!

When Phae turned up at the Lusaka Ministry of Education interview office, an English expatriate told him that the position he had applied for had already been filled. A letter should have been sent to Phae in Maseru informing him of this development, but it had apparently never been mailed. Was this British colonial incompetence or malice?

With the Lusaka job failure staring him in the face, Phae decided on a radical course of action: shelf Pan Africanism and apply for a graduate studies scholarship in the United States and admission to the prestigious Georgetown University—an institution whose product, Richard P. Stevens, PhD, had profoundly influenced Phae's views on the black-white divide. Hopefully, by the time Phae would complete his postgraduate studies, Africa would be ready to welcome qualified, black, South African staff.

With Dick Stevens's and other Americans' help, Phae's applications for both Georgetown admission and a complete U.S. scholarship were smooth and successful. He was expected at Georgetown at the beginning of the 1964–65 academic year. With a U.S. complete scholarship and a Georgetown admission letter, Phae's application for a U.S. visa at the Johannesburg consulate was smooth.

Knowing that his departure for Georgetown in August 1964 was a certainty, Phae decided to have a last fling in Bophelong. This time, though, he was not going to use his usual Maseru-Johannesburg transportation means—trains. No, this time a South African-born friend of Phae's who was living in Maseru, Desmond Sixishe, posing as a native of Basotholand, had offered to provide a car for transportation. Phae would pay for gas and other small expenses. When Phae left Maseru on this trip, he decided, uncharacteristically, to use his international rather than local passport as his primary means of identification. The local passport, with fewer visa entries, would have sufficed. At the border post, South African security details granted them a few days stay until the end of April 1964.

After a fabulous stay in Johannesburg, the two drove down south to Bophelong where both had fantasy-quality shebeen sexual experiences under the tender hands of Ciskei—a local shebeen queen.

They left Bophelong for Maseru on the last day of April. They arrived at the Maseru border post five minutes before the border was scheduled to close. For reasons Phae and Desmond couldn't fathom, the border guards wouldn't allow them to move from South Africa into Lesotho while their South African visas were still valid.

The two were forced to stay overnight in their car. Not surprisingly, there were no bathrooms or other convenience facilities for the "naturelle" or natives—the official designation of blacks in apartheid South Africa—on this side of the border. The next morning when the gates opened, Desmond was ordered to park his car while the police searched it. To Phae and Desmond's knowledge, nothing sensitive—let alone injurious—to South Africa's security was found in the car.

When the search of the car was completed, the next stage of security search for incriminating data became the passports and the visas. Today was the first of May; the two had overstayed their welcome and were now in South Africa illegally. More serious than the expiration dates of the visas, one of the South African security details "discovered" that Phae had been to Kano—most likely a city in communist, anti-apartheid Soviet Russia! It never occurred to the detail that Kano was in Nigeria and not the Soviet Union. The officer who thought Kano was in the Soviet Union came to one conclusion: this Phae guy must be a communist! He must be locked up, investigated, and prosecuted. If found guilty, he would be the officer's first victim for long-term detention, or he would be dispatched to that notorious island off the Cape Town coast.

Phae did not know the full charges until the day he appeared in front of an Afrikaner judge weeks later. Until their court appearance, Phae and Desmond were locked up incommunicado—they could not communicate with anyone outside the prison walls.

Torture at the Ladybrand prison was not heinous, much to Phae's surprise, even though he was knocked with a hard object during one brutal questioning session and suffered some brain damage. Probably the most annoying arsenal in the security crews' hands was the denial of quality sleep; security guards took pains to make sure detainees had little to no sleep. The next most annoying item was the uncovered portable toilet in the middle of the small cell, which was emptied only once a day!

The trial at Ladybrand was routine and uneventful. The judge dismissed the charges as groundless after discovering that Kano was not in the Soviet Union. After discharge, both Phae and Desmond drove straight to Maseru, where Simon Phamotse showed Phae a clipping from the Johannesburg Bantu World announcing their arrest. When Phae saw the article dated May 1, 1964, he was relieved. His parents and friends in Bophelong must certainly have seen the article. They would have suspected the final outcome of the trial. What was at issue for them was not the final outcome, but the duration of the process; the system had been known to stretch this out for months—even years!

Chapter 13

Phae's postimprisonment days in Maseru were tense and filled with a desperate sense of haste to exit southern Africa before the apartheid security apparatus could find an excuse to jail him again.

With weeks left before his departure to Georgetown, Washington D.C., Phae tried unsuccessfully to prioritize and complete his predeparture chores. These included facilitating the administrative details associated with his status as a departing student body president of the Lesotho and Pius XII College International Student Union Representative Council. The best Phae could do was to dispatch a letter through the regular mail to the executive committee of the student body that outlined his reasons for resigning and wished the incoming executive a comparatively conflict-free era characterized by courteous and respectful coexistence between the Rhodesians and the rest of the student body.

Phae also pleaded for the executive to grant Timothy Zwane, from Swaziland, the presidency of the union. The executive of the student union never replied to Phae's letter. Phae suspected that the new university administration must have intervened in the affairs of the student council, including censoring its mail. With no reply from the executive, Phae was forced to leave relevant files and office equipment with the Manyeli family.

Phae's amorous connections suffered a fate not too dissimilar to the one that marked his parting with the student council executive. He did not celebrate any final dates or have any amorous, passionate farewell encounters. Why? His virgin Basotholand Catholic girlfriend, Ntsubise, a beauty resident just outside Maseru, was in Ghana on a government scholarship. All that Phae could do was pack some of the beautiful black-and-white pictures she had sent from Ghana. Before packing them, Phae took an impassioned look at them and then implored God and his ancestors to bless her.

A girlfriend whom Phae deeply cared for, Elizabeth Ngee Kgosana of Sharpeville, couldn't be directly contacted before Phae's departure thanks to the primitive communication methods of the time. In the 1960s in Lesotho and South Africa, private residential telephone lines for black people were nonexistent and mail deliveries were unreliable, thanks to an obsession with security mail searches.

Contacting blood relatives was riddled with another complication—the fear that the South African secret police would interrupt, via an elaborate underground network, all potential communication. With the post-Sharpeville Massacre mounting international criticisms of apartheid, all those suspected of having suspicious contacts with the likes of Phae often ended up being incarcerated for indefinite periods in apartheid South Africa's horrendous prisons. Is it any wonder then that Phae's parents were not informed of the details of Phae's departure from Johannesburg's Jan Smuts Airport en route to Georgetown University?

Uninformed of the specifics of Phae's departure, none of his friends or relatives turned up at the Jan Smuts airport to bid him good-bye on that crucial evening in August 1964. At the airport, Phae was tense. The tension did not ease until after the London-bound plane had cleared the departure lanes and was soaring 30,000 feet above the South African landscape.

With South Africa far below him, Phae ordered a double Scotch whiskey—the only relaxant of which his father approved. Never had a glass of whiskey tasted so good or been so openly enjoyed!

Calm and relaxed, Phae felt comfortable enough to reach out to the passenger next to him. The passenger, an Israeli Jew now living in South Africa, turned out to be a godsend. It turned out that the

Israeli Jew was passionately anti-apartheid. His parents, who were residing in Johannesburg, were pro-ANC (African National Congress) and had participated in several anti-apartheid demonstrations in the Johannesburg area. His name, Rafi, was unfamiliar to Phae, and his color was a compromised whiteness, meaning he was white but still did not meet the typical standard of the area for "white." When Rafi heard of Phae's involvement with an international voluntary work camp led by a Jewish couple in Lesotho during the South African summer vacations of 1963, Rafi exclaimed: "This is incredible! You won't believe this; I know that couple. And more than knowing them, I have with me some pictures they took during that memorable, unprecedented Basotholand work camp season."

"Rafi!" Phae blurted out, attracting the attention of other passengers. "That's impossible!"

"Wait!" Rafi half-whispered, as he stood to reach for his traveling case. Within minutes, he had located the photo collection and was frantically searching for the pictures.

He found them.

Not only were there the pictures of the Jewish couple who had led the camp, but some of them showed Phae and Seodi Molema, the Pius XII College student Phae had had a short-lived affair with. Upon seeing Seodi's picture, Phae exclaimed, "That's impossible. That picture is of Seodi. Wait, the second picture—the one showing campers and some of their Basotho admirers and camp-related volunteers at the entrance to a cave—includes me." With mounting emotions, Phae declared, "That's me!"

Rafi was stunned. Nothing like this had ever happened to him before. He thought it was fantastic that he was sitting next to a person who had had an incredibly life-transforming experience in a voluntary work camp in a remote Basotho village with fellow Jews he knew. At that unforgettable work camp, Phae and his co-campers erected a dependable, sustainable, zero-energy-utilizing water supply system for the Basotho villagers. And for Rafi, not only to have heard of that camp session but to have known its leadership and to now have the related pictures at a crucial moment was stranger than fiction. When Rafi finally calmed down, he made a request that Phae was ready to grant.

"Don," Rafi said, "can you please describe to me in some detail your first few days at that camp, including how you overcame the lack of bathroom facilities and how you converted a Basotho mountain slope into a viable camp with running, domestic-use water?"

Phae took a good look at Rafi, smiled, and then slowly began narrating his story.

Chapter 14

Phae's arrival in New York City was without incident, even with immigration and customs. He met all the requirements for entry into the United States. Within minutes after his arrival, he placed a call to the New York City office of the African-American Institute, the key coordinator of the Southern African State Department scholarship program. The Institute gave him directions, enabling him to knock at the doors of the Institute's offices less than an hour after the call.

The staff at the African-American Institute exhibited extreme delight upon meeting Phae and spared no effort in making his arrival a happy and memorable event, including advancing him some petty cash to ease his entry. After the warm welcome, the staff gave Phae detailed advice on how to get to Washington D.C. and Georgetown, including suggesting an initial stay of a few days at the Washington D.C. YMCA while he looked for long-term accommodations.

After several days' stay at the YMCA, Phae's contact at the Africa Desk in the State Department suggested he check out the International Student House in the 1800th block of R Street. That simple suggestion proved invaluable. At the International Student House, the staff and residents—the latter were all students from abroad—welcomed Phae with a warmth he had rarely encountered in exile.

Among the warm-welcoming international students was a

Jamaican girl destined to be Phae's friend for the rest of his stay at the International Student House and for many years beyond. Phae affectionately nicknamed her, "Miss Ja," pronounced as two letters, "J.A." Jamaicans usually use "Ja" as an abbreviation for Jamaica, even in casual conversation. "Miss Ja" was a blessing in several ways, including instilling in Phae the absolute necessity of prioritizing. One of the first questions she asked Phae was simple and direct. "Don, which university did you say you were accepted at?"

"Georgetown!" Phae excitedly replied.

"Miss Ja" seemed to be pleasantly surprised. Her response, however, successfully hid the level of her surprise. "That's a highly rated university. For you to have been admitted to the Georgetown Graduate School, you must have had an impressive undergraduate record and contacts within the Georgetown community," she said.

Phae was simultaneously surprised and impressed by "Miss Ja's" reaction and its insightfulness.

"Yes!" Phae replied with controlled enthusiasm, adding, "I completed my BA at a Catholic university college in a tiny, mountainous kingdom known as Basotholand in the middle of South Africa. The college, then known as Pius XII University College, had an academic staff that was almost exclusively from either the United States or Canada. The primary financiers of the college were the Canadian Oblates, a Catholic order. I established a relationship with one member of the staff that filled my years at Pius XII with excitement and almost unbelievable adventures across the length and breadth of sub-Saharan Africa. Those with interest in African issues might have come across some of the articles he frequently submitted to the pro-Africa publications.

"His name is Dr. Richard Paul Stevens, a Georgetown PhD graduate. His insightful doctoral dissertation—Israel's relationships with the United States from its birth at the end of World War II—positioned him for several invitations to testify during congressional hearings affecting the Middle East."

"That explains it!" the sole member of his audience exclaimed, adding, "You're an extremely lucky guy to have met and known somebody with those credentials in the cauldron of southern African politics. Before you tell me more, please answer for me one question. Are you enrolled at Georgetown for the 1964–65 academic year?"

"No!" Phae replied to the pointed question, adding, "I just arrived this week and I do not even know where Georgetown is, let alone to have completed my registration paperwork."

"Glad you told me," she replied. Continuing, she said, with marked concern, "I hate to tell you. You are a few weeks late for this semester. I strongly suggest on Monday that you go straight to Georgetown to get yourself registered."

"Thanks! You can bet on it. Come Monday, I will be knocking on the doors of the Graduate School admissions office." Something in Phae's tone suggested to Miss Ja that he felt guilty about not having made this a top priority immediately after his arrival.

"Great!" Miss Ja responded before commenting: "If you do not have an appointment or commitment this afternoon, I could show you the bus route to Georgetown. Better still ..." she paused, scratched her forehead, and added affirmatively, "I will go with you. For one thing, I'm free this afternoon, and," she added, "after seeing Georgetown we could visit my university, Howard, which is not too far from where we are now."

"Oh!" Phae exclaimed, adding, "that will be really wonderful! You're truly an intriguing person. I hope one day you will give me a chance to reciprocate."

Miss Ja paused, looked at Phae with benign amusement, and added, "Don't worry, dear Don, I'll make sure I give you more than one chance to reciprocate." Concluding, she said, " Now, why don't we meet by the front entrance at 2 pm?" Phae nodded in agreement.

At two, Phae descended the International Student House stairway on his way to the front entrance. There, waiting in angelic patience, was Miss Ja, looking supremely beautiful in her Caribbean casuals.

The bus trip to Georgetown was simple and direct. Phae loved the Georgetown environs; they had the quiet solidity of an old English conservative neighborhood. Something in the layout and architecture reminded Phae of the English colonial heritage scattered all over the old, colonial Cape Town landscape.

Late registration was smoother than Phae had expected. One development, however, surprised him; all his classes were in the evenings!

When Phae turned up for his first Monday-evening class, he was beaming with confidence and anticipation. Monday's lecture was a continuation of a lecture that had been given previously, placing Phae at a disadvantage in terms of understanding some of the issues involved, especially since discussions were defined by the texts that had been previously recommended and read by most of the discussion's participants. Fortunately for Phae, he knew enough about America's diplomatic history not to be totally lost.

Several aspects of Phae's first exposure to a discussion in an American graduate class of the American colonies' search for diplomatic support during the early years of their struggle for independence stood out.

First, the atmosphere of the lecture/discussion session was open, congenial, and participatory. This was in sharp contrast to the Pius XII lecture sessions, where the lecturer delivered a formal lecture with the class's participation limited to answering mostly lecturer-generated questions.

At the end of the session, Phae received his first assignment: a critical assessment of America's diplomatic initiatives in Paris, France, during the American War of Independence. Phae undertook the assignment with unprecedented enthusiasm. The very next day, he spent hours at the Library of Congress acquainting himself with relevant primary data sources, including what would become his favorite, John Adams's letters, pamphlets, and diary.

The atmosphere at the Library of Congress was unlike any that Phae had ever encountered in libraries. For the first time in his life, Phae felt empowered beyond belief. At this magnificently constructed and comfortable library, he was convinced that he had access to all the books and documents he would ever need for his studies. More than mere facilitated access to books and documents, Phae felt enormously pleased with the library staff, who appeared warm, courteous, and above all, professional, without any traces of the racism that was fast receding in the area.

Phae's ten-page class assignment submission essay was reminiscent of his Kilnerton years: full of gusto and passion and indisputable comfort with the subject matter. Days later, when Phae's first written submission earned him only a passing grade, he couldn't believe it! What was wrong with this well-written essay? His lecturer's answer to the question was frank and direct in its simplicity.

"Don, this is a surprisingly good English essay. What I need from you, though, is, unfortunately, a graduate-school-level history essay with references and footnotes. You clearly are not familiar with this requirement. Please see me after class so we can help you familiarize yourself with our requirements."

Phae met the lecturer after class. The lecturer gave Phae a copy of Kate Turabian's Manual for Writers, fourth edition, the text students are to follow when writing their assignments and dissertations. Phae was to keep it until he could purchase his own from the university bookstore. What became crystal clear from Phae's meeting with the lecturer was the huge divide between American college-level requirements and Pius XII University College—including the University of South Africa—in terms of the importance of the appropriate and correct citation of sources. Overcoming this divide in his academic preparedness was probably the single most outstanding hurdle that Phae had to overcome. It took him two weeks to comfortably overcome this hurdle, giving him the confidence to attend to his social life in Washington D.C.

While Phae's involvement with the social life of Georgetown was minimal to nonexistent due to the simple fact that graduate classes were scheduled in the evenings, the same could not be said of his involvement with the larger, politically aware Washington D.C. community, which had taken an unexpectedly deeper interest in the anti-apartheid struggle. This larger, politically aware liberal community included many in the State Department who felt compelled to assure anti-apartheid students in the Washington D.C. area of the United States' commitment to ending apartheid. This enabled Phae, and many others from the sub-Saharan Africa who were fighting for independence from colonial yokes, to feel not only welcome in the Washington D.C. corridors of power but to be also seen by their hosts as instruments of change in dire need of refinement.

The career bureaucrats in the State Department seemed inspired not only to help anti-apartheid freedom fighters from South Africa but also the related anticolonialism freedom fighters of sub-Saharan Africa to succeed academically by providing them not only with excellent, all-costs-included scholarships but also, subtly, refining their perceptions of the deeper nature and implications of their struggles.

To assure immediate comfort for the freedom fighters, a series of carefully planned encounters with American families and liberal-minded intellectuals were organized. Some of these encounters were brief but poignant. Of the latter kind, Phae often recalls a brief encounter he had with Robert Kennedy. When Kennedy was informed that Phae was from South Africa, he looked Phae straight in the face and said, "We know about your situation in South Africa. Believe me, we are going to do something about it."

The words were simple, almost pedestrian, but the underlying passion and conviction had a remarkably intense effect on Phae. From that simple moment, Phae began to believe, with passionate intensity, that within the American corridors of power were deeply embedded, anti-apartheid liberal forces rendering the demise of apartheid a certifiable inevitability.

Feeling comfortable with America's promise politically and academically, Phae took a few minutes off to write his parents to inform them about his flight and arrival in the United States, and more importantly, about his conviction that the end of apartheid was a certainty.

"Dad," he wrote, "I have seen and touched the forces that are going to assure that justice is granted to the people of South Africa soon. Your deepest hopes for our beloved country are going to be granted—and sooner than most would suspect."

To protect his father and other family members against charges of complicity in his escape, Phae made profuse apologies for leaving South Africa without the family's knowledge or permission. The letter was delivered fourteen days later by special airmail delivery to Phae's father's store. The letter bore poorly disguised evidence of having been tampered with. The deliveryman was not a postman but a white security operative embedded with the South African Police. Needless to say, Phae didn't receive a response from his parents until years later.

*Faces of the future: Nelly Tsolo's graduation, with a
diploma in Mechanical Engineering*

Faces of the future: Ntlapu Tsolo, Molupe and Gemmina's daughter,
a born-again university graduate

Glossary

Afrikaans: The language of the descendants of the Dutch who landed in what is now the Cape Province of South Africa in 1652 and have lived there continuously ever since.

Afrikaner: One who is a descendant of the Dutch who landed in South Africa in 1652, who is visibly certifiably a Caucasian and who speaks Afrikaans.

Apartheid: Official government policy of racial segregation practiced in South Africa before 1994.

Bantu: Apartheid's term for black people.

Bantustans: Remote areas in South Africa during apartheid days designated exclusively for defined tribal groups.

Basotho: The people of what used to be called the British Commonwealth Protectorate, Basotholand, which is now Lesotho.

Bophelong: A township initially intended exclusively for black occupation, located outside Vanderbijl Park, south of Johannesburg.

CPR: Cardio-Pulmonary Resuscitation—a strictly defined system of first-aid intervention.

Kaffir: A derogatory, aggressive term for black people used by Afrikaners during apartheid days. Its usage in contemporary South Africa is illegal. The term originally meant one who didn't believe in Christianity.

Lesotho: A small, mountainous, independent state in the middle of the Republic of South Africa. It was previously called Basotholand.

Mosotho: A resident of Lesotho. Residents (plural) is Basotho.

"Me" (pronounced "Mme"): Sesotho (the language of the Basotho) word for mom/mother.

Naturelle: Literally, "naturals." During apartheid, this was one of the derogatory references to black people used by the Afrikaner.

Ntate: Word meaning "daddy" in Sesotho.

Passes: ID documents that blacks over the age of sixteen were required to possess, under apartheid, whenever they were outside of designated tribal areas. To be caught by police without this document resulted in automatic imprisonment.

Reference Book: Same as "passes" above.

Shebeens: Dynamic social institutions that were the equivalent to speakeasies in the United States, which were illegal under apartheid. They were creative responses to apartheid's refusal to allow normal recreational and social outlets in black areas. Typically, only adults patronized shebeens.

Tsirela: A black township north of Sharpeville, within the Vanderbijl Park jurisdiction.

Verwoerd, Hendrik Frensch: The architect of South Africa's apartheid policy. The hate engendered by his policies is assumed by many to have led to his assassination.

Voortrekker: Afrikaners who emigrated out of the British Colonial Cape Province in the 1830s. Most black/white conflicts were attributed to this movement.